The
Working
Border Collie

TS-287

The Publisher wishes to acknowledge the photographers who contributed to this volume: Diane Allevato, Sara Bagg, Katie Banks, Susan Bulanda, D. Burns, Greg Carleton, Wendy Carleton, Jim Clanin, Karen Clanin, Barbara Collins, J. Costello, Tim Fearon-Jones, Margay Ferguson, Isabelle Francais, Derick Garnier, Mike Godsil, Carol Harding, Victoria Hayes, Marc Henrie, Julie-Ann Holmes, Connie Jacobs, Pat Jensen, Claire Jones, Dorothy Kasper, Ray Kennedy, Ky Kindberg, William Kohler & Associates, Eric Luke, E. Luttier, Jennifer Maginnis, Joseph Mayer, Rebecca Mayer, Thomas R. McDonnell, Martha McHardy, Kevin Meyers, Moloney Studios, Simon Mosse, F. Moyes, John Muzyka, Mignon Naegeli, Brita Nybery, Padraig O'Flannabhra, Terry O'Rourke, Noreen Parrel, Jane Porter, Carole L. Presberg, David Presberg, Diana Quarton, Marjorie Quarton, R. Quill, Elaine Reinhold, Gloria Smith, Robert Smith, Karen Taylor, Scott Thom, John Thomas, Leslie Tokar, Michael Tokar, Gloria Vence, and Christine Walker.

The Working Border Collie

Marjorie Quarton
with Carole L. Presburg

Dedication

This book is dedicated to the memory of my husband John.

Marjorie

Acknowledgements

The author and publisher are grateful to the International Sheepdog Society and to the Kennel Club for permission to reproduce their materials.

Thanks are also due to the following for permission to reproduce copyright photographs: Mrs. B. Beaumont, Tim Fearon-Jones, Marc Henrie, J.A. Holmes, Ky Kindberg, J.K. and E.A. McFarlane, P. McGann, S. Mosse, F. Moyes, G. Power, Diana Quarton, and D. Quill. Every effort has been made to trace copyright owners but in some cases this has not been possible.

Contents

Crannagh Ben at work on the author's farm in Ireland.

Part One:
The Border Collie
in the British Isles

Introduction

I farmed without a working dog for twenty years. This developed in me a fine turn of speed, a profound dislike of sheep, and a nasty temper. For all those years I chased after cattle and sheep, neither owning a sheepdog nor wanting to. It simply never crossed my mind. Horses were my life, and, if I thought about it at all, I dismissed the idea of buying a working dog in the belief that I wouldn't be able to manage one anyway.

None of my neighbours had a working dog. Some owned what was called an 'old shep dog' which was usually to be found sitting on the doorstep. These dogs, heavily built, rough coated and usually brown and white but sometimes black and white or yellow, would bring in cows at a pinch but were too slow and too rough for sheep. Most of them barked non-stop when working. This type of dog, probably descended from the same ancestors as the Border Collie, seems to be on the way out. Rather sad, as they had their uses, and could be relied on not to get into mischief.

Most farmers depended on their families for help with sheep or cattle. 'Wait until the kids come home from school,' they said, if there was shearing or dipping to be done. Today's children see no fun in rounding up stock in their spare time, and, if you've ever tried to round up a bunch of yearling heifers without a dog, you will understand why.

Like myself, all those years ago, too many farmers base their knowledge of working farm dogs on sheepdog trials, or, for the last ten years, on television. They feel that a good dog is like a good racehorse—too fine an instrument for the ordinary handler. Some are sure that these dogs can't be worked without a whistle, and think the whole thing is beyond them. Others are certain that pure-bred dogs are unsuitable for cattle.

Buying your first working dog is rather like buying your first car. You wonder whether you will pass your driving test and whether you can afford petrol and insurance. 'Never mind,' you say, 'I shan't be using it much.' Then the car breaks down. Horrors! Get it fixed quickly! A return to the old bike isn't to be thought of.

So take your time when you buy your first working dog or puppy. You are unlikely to be without one in the future. You should take every opportunity to watch good farm dogs at work and talk to their owners. It's easy to make a mistake if you have to buy at short notice, and it is important to be clear in your own mind about what you, personally, look for in a dog. So many authors of practical books have been brought up with the animal they write about. They 'can't remember their first dog,'

Puppies should be handled from an early age. Marjorie Quarton with six-week-old puppies sired by Crannagh Chip.

or were working sheep with old Shep as soon as they could toddle.

When I started to write articles about working Border Collies, I had about twelve years' experience with the breed, and felt at a disadvantage among the old hands. Since then, I have changed my mind; the experience of a lifetime isn't everything. Somebody brought up from babyhood on a farm where top class dogs are taken for granted is liable to take them for granted too.

Nobody today would write about the wonders of television or air travel, because most of us have grown up with these modern marvels. We may not understand how they work, but we are used to them and assume that everyone else is too.

When I wrote a readers' queries column in the *Irish Farmers' Journal*, I was amazed not only by the response but by the basic nature of many of the questions, although most of my correspondents were experienced farmers. Answering these queries, I began to feel there was a need for a book about Border Collies.

I suppose that most readers of a book on working dogs are in search of information on how to breed, train and work their dogs with the minimum of trouble and expense. Before going any further, I want to make a point about this understandable aim. You may be efficient, knowledgeable and prepared to take some pains, but unless you are a natural dog handler, not every dog will be suitable for you.

Most owners prefer nicely marked puppies.

No two dogs are alike. Border Collies outside the show ring have not been bred for a uniform appearance, and their temperaments differ as much as their looks. If you and your dog have different temperaments, life will be harder for both of you, and you should bear this in mind when buying a dog or choosing a puppy. Compatible temperaments in man (or woman) and dog are important and may mean the difference between a happy working partnership lasting ten or twelve years, and a constant battle of wills which may spoil the dog and will certainly make the owner wish he'd taken more time in choosing his helper.

Compatible temperaments between owner and dog lead to a harmonious relationship.

I have tried to emphasize the pleasure of owning a well-trained Border Collie, as well as the economical and practical advantages. When writing any sort of specialist book, there is a strong temptation to generalise. 'The dog,' we are told, 'will then run out in a wide half circle to the right, and turn in behind the sheep.' Will he? He might. Or he might cross over in front of the sheep and turn in from the left; he might run straight down the middle of the field, or he might even run home. So much depends on you, the dog, the stock you are working, and half a dozen other things.

I read an article recently which told how much food to give 'an adult Border Collie' in grammes. I have weighed a good many Border Collies for dosing purposes, and have known an adult bitch to weigh as little as 22 lb and an adult dog as much as 60 lb. The weights are roughly halved if you deal in kilos (1 kilo = 2 lb 3 $^1/_4$ oz).

When giving information of this sort, it is extremely hard not to generalise. Even if you are specific and say 'so much food to 20 lb bodyweight,' you can still be miles out. Dogs' appetites vary; some require more nourishment than others; there are dozens of variations. Whatever you recommend is certain to be wrong for some and right for others. The same goes for training.

What I have written is the fruit of almost thirty years' experience of working Border Collies. I have tried to give practical information without going into a mass of confusing detail. For instance, if I recommend a diet, I'm not saying it's the best there is. I mean that it is readily available, I have used it for my own dogs, and it has kept them fit and healthy without costing a fortune.

My husband John introduced me to Border Collies. He came to live in Ireland after farming for many years in Yorkshire, and one of the first things he asked me was, 'Where can I get a good sheepdog?' I hadn't an idea, and we spent weeks driving hundreds of miles to see dogs which were advertised for sale. I thought some of them were pretty good, but John was hard to please. Finally he bought a handsome eighteen-month-old pedigree Border Collie called Roy.

Funny-coloured puppies get left until last. The author with Crannagh Jack.

Roy was more than half-spoiled when we got him. I distrusted him and left him to John. Not for anything would I have taken him out. John trained Roy to be a marvelous all-rounder. We kept him until he died aged twelve, and he taught me to appreciate a good dog. Gentle as a lamb with children, he had a short way with tramps. The youngest lamb was safe with him, but no bullock questioned him twice.

I shall never forget my first attempt to work Roy. John was away, and a dozen cattle broke into the garden which was my mother's pride and joy. I took Roy on a lead, thinking the sight of him might help. A moment later, he jerked the chain out of my hand, rounded up the cattle and took them back to the field with the minimum of help from me. I remember shouting 'Sit down!' at the top of my voice, and being surprised and delighted when he obeyed.

A picture of health. Meg is a brood bitch in peak condition.

It was some time before I dared risk trying to work sheep with Roy—he'd been so rough with them as a young dog—but he did everything I asked. From that time, I was a convert to working Border Collies and bought a bitch for myself.

Since then I have come to know these wonderful dogs well and to appreciate them at their true worth. A good working dog saves time, labor and money. He is helper, guard and friend. A pedigree Border Collie can also be a source of extra income in the form of stud fees and puppies. Be sure though that other people share your opinion before embarking on a breeding programme. It's easy to be prejudiced in favor of your own dog.

Without a natural 'way' with dogs, you can't hope to reach the top in sheepdog trials or to work difficult dogs in difficult conditions. Anyone, and I mean anyone, can use a dog for farm work, provided that the dog has the necessary ability and that he and his master are temperamentally suited to one another.

An expert handler can deal with any sort of dog, but even he is certain to have a favorite type—that which complements the handler's own nature. Such a team can achieve feats of stockmanship together which neither could do without his ideal partner.

Origins and History
of the Breed

EARLY DAYS

Nobody knows for certain when dogs were first trained to earn their living. Long ago, perhaps, some caveman's child kept an orphaned puppy for a pet and brought it up as we might a fox cub. It is all speculation, and although dogs' bones have been found along with human remains in ancient settlements and cave dwellings, we can only guess at the part those dogs played in the lives of the humans of prehistoric days.

All domestic creatures have been tamed and improved with the benefit of man in mind, whether it is to produce meat, wool or milk, to lay eggs or to keep down vermin and guard property. In all probability, the first domestic dogs were guard dogs whose aggressive instincts were shaped to human use. The earliest pictures of dogs, in caves, on canvas and carved in sculpture, show them helping man to hunt down his quarry.

Wild dogs hunt in packs and must hunt in order to survive. The tamed dog would be induced, willingly or otherwise, to share his kill with the family. They were also most likely kept as pets, for the taming of wild creatures has been popular for thousands of years. Not only dogs and cats, but songbirds, monkeys and even snakes have been tamed and kept as household pets.

The first 'sheepdogs' were savage creatures whose function was to protect their masters' flocks from wild animals and human marauders rather than to herd them. It would be interesting to know the story of the first exasperated shepherd who thought of training the hunting instinct of his dog so as to gather his sheep and goats and to fetch or drive them on command.

Wild dogs round up helpless animals such as sheep in order to single one out and kill it for food. Today when a number of stray dogs get together, they revert to their old way of life, and do exactly this. It must have occurred to some observant dog lover centuries ago that, if a single dog could be trained to head off a flock of sheep on his own and stop when told, the sheep could be penned unharmed in folds.

Of all domestic animals, the dog serves the most purposes, and of all dogs the Border Collie is surely the most versatile.

THE SHEPHERD'S DOG IN HISTORY AND LITERATURE

It took hundreds of years for working Border Collies as we know them today to evolve, and they had been earning their living for centuries before they came by their name.

The Collie breed has split up into five breeds today, the Rough Collie, the Smooth, the Shetland Sheepdog, the Bearded Collie (or 'Beardie' as he is often called) and the Border Collie. There are many other types of herding dog scattered all over the world, some are collies, some are not.

J.J. Templeton with Roy, a dog whose name is known to everyone involved with Border Collies.

The Australian Kelpie, although not called a collie, is said to descend from smooth-coated black and tan Border Collies exported from Scotland during the last century. There are also local breeds, such as the Wicklow Collie in Ireland, which are a type rather than a breed and often come from a strain of unregistered Border Collies.

By definition, a sheepdog is one that works with sheep. He is not necessarily a collie. In some countries 'sheepdogs' are still required to protect their charges from wild animals.

Back in 1570, Dr. John Caius, Physician-in-Chief to Queen Elizabeth, published in Latin a classification of 'British dogs'. This was translated a few years later, and shepherds' dogs were included in the same section as mastiffs and bulldogs. Dr. Caius gave such a striking description of the working sheepdog that it is quoted, at least in part, in almost every work about the breed. I have come across it so often that I am tempted to omit it. However, the picture it gives, after four hundred years, is still so accurate that it will stand repetition.

'This dogge, either at the hearing of his master's voyce, or at the wagging and whisteling in his fist, or at his shrill and hoarse hissing, bringeth the wandring weathers and straying sheepe into the self same place where his master's will and wishe is to have them, whereby the shepherd reapeth this benefite, namely, that with little labour and no toyle or moving of his feete he may rule and guide his flocke, according to his owne desire, either to have them go forward, or to stand still, or to drawe backward, or to turne this way or to take that way. For it is not in Englande as it is in Fraunce, as it is in Flaunders, as it is in Syria, as it is in Tartaria, where the sheepe follow the shepherd, for heere in our country, the shepherd followeth the sheepe. And sometimes the straying sheepe, when no dogge runneth before them, gather themselves together in a flocke when they hear the shepherd whistle in his fist, for feare of the dogge (as I imagine) remembering this (if unreasonable creatures may be reported to have memory) that the dogge commonly runneth out at his master's warrant which is his whistle. This have we often times diligently marcked in taking our journey from towne to towne. When we have heard a shepherd whistle, we have rayned in our horse and stood styll a space to see the proofe and trial of this matter. Furthermore with this

Strong dogs are usually "cool" with the herd. A strong dog never backs down.

dogge doth the shepherd take sheepe for ye slaughter and to be healed if they be sicke, no hurt or harme in the world done to the simple creature.'

If we ignore the archaic phrasing and spelling of this remarkable piece, we might suppose it to have been written yesterday by a townsman, unfamiliar with working dogs and their handlers. It is a pity that Dr. Caius didn't describe the appearance of the dogs he found so absorbingly interesting to watch, contenting himself with saying that they were of indifferent size. This tells us little, as he doesn't specify what type of dog he is comparing them with.

If others wrote of the shepherd's dog at work during the next two

Border Collies are normally calm, sensible dogs with good herding ability.

centuries their writings have not survived. Possibly the reason for the silence about sheepdogs lies with the old social order. Sheepdogs belonged to shepherds rather than to their employers. Certainly writers before 1800 mentioned shepherds (and shepherdesses as well) but these were more given to dalliance than to any actual work if the poets are to be believed.

The early writers about working dogs were working men. James Hogg, the Ettrick Shepherd, wrote a touching story called 'Duncan Campbell, or the Faithful Dog.' The dog, Oscar, a collie, is treated with a casual cruelty by almost everyone except his master; the story shows how little working dogs were considered in those days. Hogg also wrote often of his own collies, Sirrah and Hector, in the early 1800s, showing a love and understanding all too rare at the time.

Earlier, the poet Wordsworth had written:
Waving his hat, the Shepherd in the vale
Directs his winding dog the cliffs to scale,
That, barking busy, mid the glittering rocks
Hunts where he points the intercepted flocks.

Border Collies differ from other working Sheepdogs in that they usually work in silence. Perhaps it is poetic licence.

DEVELOPMENT OF THE BREED

Queen Victoria's fondness for collies gave them a real boost. Overnight, a fine collie became a status symbol, as did the Corgi in the present century. The Royal collies were painted by the most famous artists of the day. They had become fashionable. Around 1860, they started to appear in dog shows, and Old Mec and Old Cockie marked the split whence came the Rough Collie, sometimes called the 'Lassie type', so popular ever since. One of Queen Victoria's own dogs Gypsie, was shown in the 1860s. She was mainly black, and would pass today as a pedigree Border Collie. As a show animal, she would not be considered. We can take it that the Border Collie is the original breed from which today's Rough Collies have split off. The latter have been bred taller, with great emphasis on a fine coat, with long narrow faces, and importance being attached to colour.

The collies which were not moulded to a particular standard continued as before to be bred for work and work only.

Certainly there have been infusions of blood from other breeds, but so there has in the Rough Collie. In the case of the Border, outside blood was introduced only when it was considered that it would improve the working performance.

One of the reasons why thoroughbreds are generally better than crossbreds is that good purebred working dogs are not mated with other breeds unless by accident. Owners of valuable dogs don't care to experiment with their stock, so animals which are deliberately crossed are usually those which aren't considered good enough for pure breeding.

Today's Border Collies can all be traced to a handful of distinguished forbears, but there is no doubt that other elements have been introduced from time to time when it was thought that this would improve working performance.

The power of the eye to control stock is the working quality peculiar to Border Collies. Some dogs work adequately without 'eye'. They are then said to be 'plain' or 'loose-eyed'. The 'strong-eyed' Border Collie at work bears a distinct resemblance to the gundog pointing game. Many authorities believe that 'eye' was bred into the Border Collie from setters, but it is likely that spaniels and pointers were also used.

This quality has been around in sheepdogs for two hundred years or more. Back in 1790, James Hogg, mentioned earlier, wrote the following about his dog:

'Whenever (the dog) was within doors, his whole occupation was watching and pointing the cat from morning to night. When she flitted

Concentration: The late Dougie Little from The Isle of Man with Mirk.

from one place to another, so did he in a moment; and then squatting down he kept his point sedulously till he was either called off or fell asleep.'

These words still apply to any keen young Border Collie with an interest in stock. I have seen puppies six weeks old or even less, heads and tails lowered, creeping up to cats and poultry, then remaining as if transfixed for minutes at a time.

In some cases there is a 'chicken and egg' situation with regard to sheepdogs and gundogs. A shepherd who worked on the Gordon Castle estate owned a collie bitch which was equally good at pointing game and gathering sheep. As a result, the Duke of Gordon used to ask the shepherd to join shooting parties with his dog. She had a wonderful nose, and often found game when other dogs had failed. As the shepherd refused to sell his bitch, the Duke persuaded him to have her mated with a setter. The resulting progeny were the first Gordon Setters.

In Peebleshire, around 1934, a farmer with a good working Border Collie bitch of trial standard, mated her on at least two occasions with a liver and white spaniel of cocker type. The puppies, mostly coloured like their father, had their mother's herding ability. Although there is no record of their having run in trials, they were excellent working dogs, both with sheep and cattle.

There can be little doubt that sheepdogs and gundogs have been interbred in the past by gamekeepers and shepherds who were trying to breed a dual purpose dog. Nowadays, no owner of a valuable bitch would want to experiment with cross breeding.

It is fascinating to see how gundog characteristics which have lain dormant for generations can crop up again. Border Collies can sometimes look as if they were half setter or half pointer when there is no possibility of this being the case.

We have owned at different times four dogs by the classically bred Border Collie Glenabo Lad, but from unrelated mothers. These dogs were brown, white and mottled, with large low-set ears, strong jaws and domed skulls. The sire was a black and white dog with bent over ears, wedgeshaped head and no trace of mixed ancestry. None of the three bitches responsible for the four dogs was in any way unusual to look at. These brown dogs all had more 'eye' than either parent. There was no brown dog in their pedigrees nearer than five generations back.

There are two distinct types of brown sheepdog, the foxy-red and the liver coated. The liver colour is often associated with a distinctive trotting gait, in which the hocks are scarcely bent, and the whole hind leg swings forward. I have noticed pointers and Irish Setters trotting like this.

Most (though not all) Border Collies have good noses and, if not prevented when young, will go rabbiting. This can be a great nuisance as, once established, the habit is difficult to cure. One of our best dogs, Dale, was a super worker with any stock, provided he didn't put up a hare. If he did, you had to manage without his help until he tired of the chase. This dog would set a pheasant hidden in a tuft of grass, standing in exactly the same attitude as if he were penning sheep. Incidentally, he too was by Glenabo Lad. Some handlers today use their Border Collies with the gun. One such is Barbara Beaumont, whose Bracken has been placed in a gundog event.

Obedience trials have drawn attention to the scenting and retrieving ability of the Border Collie, and I believe that, with careful breeding, a dual purpose dog could be produced if there was a demand for such an animal.

Bearded Collies appear occasionally in the annals of the Border, the best known being W.B. Telfer's Old Maddie, which must appear in most pedigrees a long, long way back. Talking of 'Beardies' though, the working Bearded Collie of the first half of the century had little in common with today's show animal. In particular the curtain of hair over the face would be out of place in a working dog.

I suspect, although I have no proof, that hill farmers have speeded up the breed by adding a dash of Whippet or Lurcher. Some present day Border Collies are thin skinned, light boned creatures which gallop like the wind and are often more highly strung than what we think of as the conventional type.

THE INTERNATIONAL SHEEP DOG SOCIETY: THE STUD BOOK

The International Sheep Dog Society was founded in July 1906 by a group of dog handlers from the Border counties.

They drew up the constitution of the Society naming its aims, of which the most important was to 'improve the breed of the collie with a view to the better management of stock.' In the same year, the first International Trial was run at Gullane Hill in East Lothian, and was won after a re-run by Richard Sandiland's Don.

As the years passed, trials became popular in a wider and wider area. The Society kept records of the breeding of dogs, and they were included in a register, but it was not until 1951 that a Stud Book was compiled. After four years' research, the Stud Book committee produced eight books, two large volumes containing 3,000 registrations each, and five slimmer books. In all, 14,000 dogs were entered. Some of the records had been lost, so the first book is not as accurate as it might have been had it been compiled sooner. The Stud Book has appeared every year since and, with registrations running at more than 6,000 a year, it is now a fat book priced dearly.

A complete set is a rare and valuable possession. The first volume, which takes us up to 1939, includes No. 9, Old Hemp, one of the greatest foundation dogs of all, Fingland Loos, 435, a great trial winner and brood bitch, G. Brown's Spot 308 who founded the breed in the U.S.A., and I. Herdman's Tommy, 16.

It has taken many generations to make the Border Collie the beautiful and intelligent dog we know today. Norman Seamark's Bill.

It is mainly through Tommy that the line of Old Hemp is handed down, and most modern pedigrees trace back to him.

No. 1 in Vol. 1 of the Stud Book is a bitch of Andrew Brown's called Old Maid, and she also founded a strong family, mainly through her daughter Old Nell, 205. This latter bitch died in 1919, aged 13 years, having produced 80 puppies!

The only dogs in Vol. 1 known to have been of a breed other than the Border Collie are W.B. Telfer's Old Maddie, No.8, a 'Beardie', and her descendants.

The Stud Book committee worked with the greatest enthusiasm to produce a true record, and the results of their work are fascinating to the student of breeding. Nowadays the words 'Border Collie' are introduced into all registration papers. A dog of mixed blood can be registered only on merit and this means stringent tests and considerable expense.

The late J.A. Reid, a solicitor from Airdrie in Scotland, was Secretary of the International Sheep Dog Society from 1915 to 1948. He was especially active in promoting the breed, and it was due to him that the name 'Border Collie' became generally used after being introduced just after World War Two.

J.M. WILSON AND HIS DOGS

One of the men to make most use of the great bloodlines in the early volumes of the Stud Book was J.M. Wilson, the greatest sheepdog handler of all time. His 'Whitehope' dogs were famous in their time, and continue to form the basis of many pedigrees today.

J.M. Wilson won 55 National and International trials, and his record of nine Supreme Championships is unlikely ever to be beaten. He competed for nineteen years, winning his first' Supreme' in 1928 with Fly. His one-eyed Roy is the only dog ever to have won three Internationals, in 1934, 1936 and 1937. J.M. Wilson's final win was with Bill in 1955. He was a practical man, and, having made a name for his dogs, he sold hundreds all over the world.

We can never be quite certain whether J.M. Wilson's genius flattered his dogs or whether they were as good as he. No doubt they were marvellous dogs, but the rush to use them at stud resulted in considerable line breeding, not all of it desirable. Some modern pedigrees are completely dominated by 'J.M's' bloodlines. This is thought by some to have helped to produce dogs which, although delightful to watch, are far softer than their forbears.

POWER: HARD AND SOFT DOGS

Here we come to the question of 'power' or the lack of it, which crops up whenever working Border Collies are discussed. The early herding dogs were hardier by far than today's specimens, they were capable of shifting the most stubborn ewe, the most aggressive bullock. Along with this went a temperament far more independent than that of the average Border Collie of today. Shepherds' dogs were often extremely savage and sometimes savagely treated.

The coming of Sheepdog Trials led to the selection of 'classy' dogs for breeding purposes. It became vital that the dog should stop instantly on command, that he run out wide so as not to alarm the small number of sheep and that he keep his distance from them. As it is far harder to work four sheep than say forty, it is essential that they should be controlled quietly - made to think they are doing as they like. It takes a good dog to work three or four sheep efficiently and without fuss. In the process of breeding good trial dogs, it must not be forgotten that most shepherds need to move large numbers of sheep at a time, or small numbers through mud or shallow water or along narrow lanes.

J.P. MacKenzie's Don, winner of the 1985 International, showing gundog influence in his attitude, paw raised, at the pen.

The dog with power can move ewes with lambs, because he does not need to attack in order to enforce his authority. Truly powerful dogs are also cool. Some powerful dogs are said to be 'hard'. This means that they are also aggressive, keen and difficult to slow up. These dogs respond to skilful handling, but are of no use to beginners. The scourge of the present day from the farmer's point of view is the 'soft' dog. He goes nicely as long as things go right for him, and is easily handled, but is over sensitive, cannot bear correction, and is cowardly if challenged by sheep or cattle.

Thirty years ago, there were fewer aids to shepherding. Dogs didn't ride in tractors or landrovers, but ran behind bicycles. Sheep were seldom housed and dogs worked in all conditons of weather. They knew nothing of balanced diets, they worked long hard hours in busy times and remained chained up when idle.

The dog's lot is more pleasant now and, like his master, he works shorter hours and lives in greater comfort. He is also much more valuable. A type of dog has been evolved as far removed from his forbears as the racehorse is from the Shire. More shepherds are interested in winning trials, they have more spare time for training their dogs and have the means to travel to competitions many miles away.

Most serious breeders and handlers are concerned about loss of stamina in today's dogs, and it is often put down to the indiscriminate breeding to International winning sires, regardless of the fact that the handler is at least partly responsible for their winnings. There is a general feeling that new bloodlines are needed, and a discontent with the average working Border Collie.

I feel sure that one of the reasons for the concentration of a few bloodlines comes from placing undue emphasis on the sire and not enough on the dam. There are a mere half dozen sire lines responsible for almost all today's leading dogs, but the forty-five-plus International Champions since the war trace to about thirty female lines. Here there is far more scope for out-crossing within the framework of the breed, and much might be achieved by reviving some of the great female lines of the past.

The Working
Border Collie Today

SHEEPDOG TRIALS

Sheepdog trials can be anything from a friendly competition between
farmers to an all-absorbing passion.

They have done a tremendous amount of good, both by establishing
the breed of modern Border Collies and by improving the skill of
handlers. They have also created much public interest in trialling as is
evident by the enormous popularity of the B.B.C. Series *One Man and His
Dog*.

Sheepdog trials have come a long way since the first recorded event
held at Bala in North Wales in 1873. In that year Lloyd Price, owner of vast
estates in the area, organised a 'Novelty' event. This was a sheepdog trial,
'Open to the World'. The entry fee was £10, a large amount in those days
and the judge was a 'tried and trusty shepherd' who was not apparently
considered worth naming in the record of the event.

Ten dogs competed, and the honours went to Scotland, the winner
being Jamie Thomson with Tweed.

From that day on, it was recognised that the only way for a farmer to
prove his dog better than his neighbour's was to match them. It seems
likely that the test then, as now, was far from settling all arguments, but
it is still the only form of working test open to sheepdogs.

'Trialling' has never really taken on as a spectator sport, television
excepted. At Bala, more than a century ago, three hundred people
watched the new novelty sport. That would be an unusually large crowd
today. Hundreds of trials are held every year, but the bulk of the
onlookers are competitors and their families plus a few addicts, victims
of the 'trial bug.' More often than not, the trials are small local affairs, held
in remote areas, sketchily advertised and with prizes which would not
begin to pay expenses even for consistent winners.

The exceptions are the National and International trials, and an
increasing number of sponsored events, and area championships.

The International Sheep Dog Society stages four National trials
annually, in England, Ireland, Scotland and Wales, competitors from the

Isle of Man competing in the Irish event. At each National trial, the best fifteen form a team to compete in the International Championship.

The 'International' is held on three days in September. On the first two days all the team members compete in a qualifying event. On the third day, the best fifteen take part in the Supreme Championship over an extended course.

Sheepdog trials are based on farm work, or to be more accurate, on the type of work done by a sheepdog on a hill farm. Not all trials are the same, but basically they consist of outrun, lift, fetch, drive, pen and shed.

The handler sends his dog anything from two to four hundred yards to fetch a small number of sheep, usually four or five. The dog has to run well out so as not to send the sheep back to the pens. He then has to fetch the sheep through a gate or pair of hurdles, steer them around the handler, drive them away through another obstacle, turn and drive them across the course, through a third set of gates, then back to a gated

A calm powerful dog: the author's Mac.

pen. After penning he must send the sheep out of the pen and drive them off the course. There is always a time limit, and equal scores are sometimes judged on time. In open competitions, the handler also has to divide or 'shed' the sheep into two groups, and hold the shed sheep so that they do not re-unite again. Sometimes the dog also has to single out a marked sheep and drive it away from the others. All these things have to be done quietly and without fuss. The handler is not allowed to touch the sheep at any time.

Every stage of the trial is derived from farm work, although it is unusual for a shepherd to have to send a dog a long way for just a few sheep at home. The trial is a sort of shop window. Working Border Collies fetch all sorts of stock long distances in far from ideal conditions on the farm. They have to work where they can't see the sheep until they are within yards of them due to rocks, bushes or uneven ground. A good dog must be able to drive sheep as well as fetch them. If there is a gap, he must be able to steer them through it without fuss, and shedding and penning are often necessary especially in lambing time.

There are two aims in a sheepdog trial. One is to prove that A has a better dog than B (or that the judge thinks he has). The avowed aim of the International Sheep Dog Society however, is to improve the breed of sheepdogs for herding by encouraging competition. It is by no means certain that this end is being achieved, as many, though by no means all, trial dogs are quite unsuited to the rough and tumble of ordinary farm work. It is disquieting to hear those in authority in the Society complaining not of unsuitable dogs but of unsuitable sheep.

It will be interesting to see whether, in days to come, 'trialling' will become a completely separate sport, unrelated to farm work. If this should happen it would be a great pity. A sheepdog trial should be as much a farmer's sport as a ploughing match, not a fancy demonstration in which suitable sheep have to be found to 'lead' the dog round the course without any fear of a confrontation.

One function of a trial is to bring home to the dogless just what a difference a good Border Collie could make.

Imagine, if you can, the sheep turned out of the pen and the dogs on strike! How many people would be needed to do what the dog does, and how long would it take them? Even a moderate dog is better than none, and the man who has owned one good one will never again be without one.

Eye: Mac, a strong-eyed dog.

Herding in the field is natural practice for the sheepdog trial.

SHOWING

Each year, over 6,000 Border Collies are registered with the International Sheep Dog Society, and an ever increasing number with the Kennel Club, which has now severed its connection with the I. S. D. S.

This book is not concerned with showing dogs, but it must be mentioned that, in order to qualify for the title of Show Champion, a Border Collie must, in addition to winning three Challenge Certificates, prove that he can work sheep.

The only dogs exempted from the tests are those which have qualified since 1982 for the National or International Sheep Dog Trials, or those which have gained a first to seventh place in an Open Sheep Dog Trial affiliated to the I.S.D.S.

The test is simple, no more than an indication that all working instinct is not lost. The pass mark is 60 per cent.

The dog must carry out the following:

Outrun, maximum distance 200 yards	20 points
Lift five sheep	10 points
A straight fetch past a post to the handler	20 points
Drive back to post, maximum 100 yards	30 points
Pen 12' x 6' with a gate	20 points
	100 points

Time allowed 15 minutes.

The Kennel Club did not accept the Border Collie breed until 1976, and Championship status was not granted until 1982. Fortunately, the breed standard seems to keep working characteristics in view, and it is to be hoped that showing enthusiasm will not allow a beautiful working breed to become a caricature as has been the case with some other working dogs.

OBEDIENCE AND AGILITY

The Border Collie and his unregistered relation the working sheepdog are today supreme in Obedience Tests. For example, the Supreme Obedience Championships at Crufts in 1985 produced 48 competitors, all champions in their own right, of which 44 were Border Collies or working sheepdogs. This trend has been apparent now for several years, and classes are having to be arranged which exclude Border Collies.

Another type of competition work at which Border Collies excel is agility. Combined with their natural obedience, the nature of their proper work ensures that they must be active. Most are very fast and enjoy jumping.

The close breeding favoured by those who breed to show can often result in undesirable characteristics cropping up. Those which, like hip dysplasia, affect the dog's agility, are soon discovered, whereas the non-working Border Collie may be an unsuspected sufferer and pass on the defect to his progeny.

Obedience and agility tests are not, properly speaking, work, so I don't intend to describe them. They are, however, activities in which working Border Collies are supreme in the U.K. The type of dog described in the last chapter which a shepherd would call 'soft' might well be a big winner in obedience, for often those dogs which lack initiative when it comes to dealing with awkward stock are the easiest to train.

A nervous or bad-tempered dog would be useless for obedience work, but properly handled, might do very well working stock. Equally, some successful 'Obedience' dogs would be considered 'fussy' by a practical farmer. Fussiness, or over-friendliness, is only partly due to a puppy's uphringing. Much of the dog's temperament is present at birth.

GUIDE DOGS FOR THE BLIND

Of recent years, Border Collies have begun to be popular guide dogs. More often than not, they are crossed with a Labrador or Golden Retriever, but a suitable purebred can make an excellent guide. The Border Collies' main fault for this work is their quick thinking and quick movement. They are seldom suitable for an elderly person, but it is a mistake to think that only the elderly and infirmed need guide dogs. A very careful selection has to be made, as the dog must come from a strain free from jealousy. A dog constantly with one person builds up a close affinity with him, whatever the breed. Close relationships can lead to jealousy, just as surely as in the human race, resulting in the dog resenting other people's efforts to help his charge and being protective to the point of aggression.

Certain strains are better than others. Some Border Collies are too small and light for the work, others would never become steady enough. Some Border Collies are too sensitive to loud noises, others tend to chase, their working instinct being still active. The type required is steady and placid, with no nervousness at all, good with people. They are, of course, reared in the house from a few weeks old, and this helps. The best are as good as anyone could wish. As guide dogs are spayed bitches or, castrated males, the breed of the best can only be perpetuated by keeping a brother or sister to breed from.

DOGS FOR MOUNTAIN RESCUE

Border Collies are also used extensively in mountain rescue work in Snowdonia and elsewhere. In order to be suitable for training for this work, the dog must be 'stockproof'. In other words, he must be completely free of the herding instinct or have had it trained out of him. The same, of course, applies to guide dogs. The Snowdonia rescue team of dogs used to consist mainly of German Shepherds. Now about half their dogs are Border Collies, the remainder being German Shepherds and Labradors. The Collies are useful because they cast out looking for the survivors of climbing accidents in exactly the same way as they would search for sheep lost in snowdrifts.

Puppies intended for mountain rescue work must be hardy.

It takes two years to train a dog for this work, and he is reassessed every three years. The dogs and their handlers have to be winched up and down from helicopters in the worst of weather conditions. As with guide dogs, bitches are preferred, and a long coat which collects mud and snow is a handicap. These dogs must be free of 'eye', friendly and alert. Like guide dogs, they are kept indoors from an early age.

In June 1984 in Scotland, a Border Collie called Glen rescued eleven schoolgirls from the hut where they'd spent the night. A party of thirty-three had set out on a Highland walk, and at 6 pm, eleven were found to be missing. The Killin and Lomond rescue team was called out, and sixteen men searched until six o'clock in the morning. As Dr. Bob Scott, one of the rescue party, was covering the ground for the second time, his dog Glen broke away from him, and made his way to 'Goblin's Cave', 300 feet up Ben Venue. The girls who had been huddled there for more than twelve hours were fifteen and sixteen years old. Some of the rescuers must have passed the place twice during the night.

Border Collies and part Borders have also been used for police and army work, as 'sniffer' dogs seeking out drugs, in circuses and in films. They have their own television series, the ever popular *One Man and His Dog*, and there is no more faithful companion.

THE BORDER COLLIE ON THE FARM

Now we come to the working Border Collie on the farm, which is, after all, his usual and rightful place.

In spite of the growing popularity of the breed, I am still often asked 'What exactly *is* a Border Collie?' The answer to this question is not as simple as it might appear. One might say: 'It is a type of collie, distinguished by silent working and the power of the eye, which dominates sheep dog trials and farm work today.' There is more to it than that. The Border Collie is, as I have already shown, half a dozen dogs rolled into one. What your working Border Collie is depends on you—what you need and how you treat him.

Border Collies are not of much interest to commercial breeders. They don't always make ideal pets, tend to produce smallish litters and are not uniform in appearance. As a result, very few people breed them in numbers, regardless of quality, in order to make a few pounds on the puppies. If they don't come from a good strain, they will be hard to sell.

"The best exercise is work." Bess takes a short cut.

The way to a pedicure or a cold bath. Dunedin Sam and Bess force reluctant lambs into a race.

This means that most litters of registered puppies have at least one good parent, and the majority are bred specifically for farm work. This work may be divided as follows.

> Work with sheep on the hills
> Work with lowland sheep
> Work with dairy cows
> Work with dry cattle
> Work with rough cattle (drovers' and dealers' dogs)
> Work loading and penning sheep: work in yards

(shearers', dealers' and contractors' dogs).

No dog can or should be expected to do all these things, but many work sheep and cattle. The dual-purpose dog is more valuable than the one which only works sheep. Some of these won't work sheep if there are cattle in the field.

THE HILL DOG

The 'hill dog' is the hardest to do without. He can travel miles in rough going where no tractor or motor bike can go. The work he does couldn't be done without him. Hill farmers usually prefer a light, fast, active dog without too heavy a coat. He may have to run over rocks, through heather and through mountain streams, casting out until he has gathered the hill sheep which, like him, are light, active and fast. Many trial dogs are of this type, and they are beautiful to watch if they are good.

They must also be tough and not cowardly—a ewe with young lambs is as obstinate as any bullock, and hill sheep have horns.

These dogs from the hills of the Border Country and the Scottish Highlands are the ones which get most attention in literature and the press. In fact, some people seem to think that, away from the hills, a sheepdog is not needed.

The first time I saw a sheepdog at work was on St. Patrick's Day at the end of the terrible winter of 1947–48. I was at school in Dublin, and had gone on a bike ride with some friends in the Dublin mountains where snow still lay thick in the ditches, and piled high in drifts under the March sun.

We were thrilled when we came across a party of men digging sheep out of a drift where they had been buried for more than a fortnight. Most of them were still alive in a round, igloo-like chamber which looked as if it were lined with brown glass, and smelled like nothing on earth.

We noticed a bedraggled sheepdog, digging frantically at the frozen snow. He whined, and his paws were bleeding. 'He's found another!' A man went to help with a spade, but the sheep was dead. Somebody remarked, 'A good dog is worth seven men'. The dog, a trial winner, had led his owner to the place where more than twenty sheep were buried.

Few of our dogs are called upon to locate buried sheep, but the hill dog, more than any of his working brothers, must show initiative as well as obedience.

We say 'How clever!' when we see dogs performing tricks within a few feet of their handlers. The hill dog is often out of sight of the shepherd; in bad weather he may be out of earshot. Faced with a problem, he must decide what to do without instruction. And he must never bite unless attacked by a ewe when he may grip her nose and let it go again. It isn't safe to allow a dog that bites to work out of sight of his handler, or he may become a killer.

One of my dogs will gently turn a sheep right way up if she has got onto her back, but a helpless sheep is a sore temptation to a dog.

The Lowland Sheepdog

Lowland sheep are bigger, heavier and slower than their relations on the hills. There are many breeds and while some are merely improved hill sheep, others are quite different in their behaviour, being obstinate and disinclined to move. This is where the calm, powerful dog comes into his own. If he is truly forceful but not rough, those sheep will turn and walk away. Another dog could not move them without flying in and snapping.

A dogless lowland sheep farmer of my acquaintance said, 'You don't need a dog—shake a bucket of nuts, and the sheep will follow you.' They will too. They will follow and surround you, and should you slip and fall, a big flock could trample you. You have no chance of sorting your sheep or counting them. One of the most important functions of a sheepdog in winter is to keep the sheep back while you put those same nuts into their troughs. You can hold a gate slightly open and count your sheep as the dog drives them through, you can divide a bunch putting some in each of two or three buildings.

If you keep a small number of sheep, a good dog makes the difference between employing a shepherd and doing without. It takes a lot of sheep to pay a shepherd's wages, and he won't work a seven day week either! With expenses at today's level, a small flock of sheep can't hope to pay if a man's wage has to come out of the profits.

Modern sheep farmers spend large sums on sheep-handling units, dipping tanks, shedding gates, races and forcing pens, all of which are designed to reduce labour. Even with the most streamlined layout, handling sheep without a dog can be an exhausting and frustrating business. Heavy adult sheep just don't like moving along between bars, knowing very well that the way leads to a cold bath or a pedicure! A dog can achieve more than two men here and will save endless time.

The Cow Dog

Some dairy farmers are horrified at the idea of allowing a dog near their high yielding milkers, but those who do use dogs wouldn't be without them. Cows are creatures of habit and need only a slight reminder to set them off on the path to the milking parlour. Dogs are creatures of habit too, and it doesn't take a very wonderful one to learn 'cow time.'

A plain barking dog will move a herd of cows used to a dog and get them up if they are lying down.

A good Border Collie can achieve more with one nip almost at ground level (the kicking hoof flies harmlessly over his head) than his noisy relation can by barking himself hoarse. A barking dog is like a shouting

Border Collie puppies are accident prone, as they don't know how to avoid trouble. Crannagh Princess at six months.

man. After a while he isn't heeded at all. The word will quickly pass from cow to cow either that the new dog is harmless or that he has sharp teeth. A good cow dog never bites any higher than the heel, except when a nip on the nose is needed.

An entirely non-aggressive dog is useless with cows. They will know at once that he is not worthy of respect and will chase him out of the field. He must be brave enough to stand his ground and nip the ringleader's nose.

Amusingly enough, some of those farmers, most indignant at the thought of rounding up their dairy cows with a dog, think nothing of walloping them with a stick. Cows have to be accustomed to fresh quarters and heifers to the milking machine. They have to be forced into crushes for veterinary treatment and into trailers to go to market. Without a dog, the farmer has to use a stick and often call in a neighbour with another stick!

The Cattle Dog

A good cattle dog needs to be keener than a cow dog. Dry cattle don't always tread the same path and may have to be moved on strange ground, loaded into trailers or fetched out of yards. Like cows, they very soon learn whether the dog is to be feared or not. Cattle are more easily rounded up by men than sheep, and it is less often necessary to gather them, so it is possible to do without a cattle dog. If, however, you have once owned a good one, you will never want to be without one again.

There is no reason at all why the same Border Collie shouldn't work cattle and sheep—many do, and do it well. The problem lies in the dog's handling. In order to move cattle, he must get right up to them, bite if necessary, and generally let them see who is boss, at least until they get to know him. The sheepdog must be restrained or he will scatter his flock all over the place. The trial dog must be curbed harder still, as he works such a small number of sheep.

Most of my dogs here work both cattle and sheep as required, but a dog which regularly works strong cattle will not stop instantly as he should when working sheep.

The Rough Cattle Dog

Any good Border Collie which is not afraid of cattle can be trained to work rough bullocks. It is a matter of urging him on and never restraining him, however savagely he goes to work.

Suckler cows are the hardest stock to shift. The very best dogs for rough cattle are the calm powerful characters I mentioned before. They are rarely found, and often thought too valuable to risk in dealer's yards or among suckler herds. Savage dogs upset the cattle and may cause them to break through fences and escape.

These dogs are less common than they were, and I have heard it said there was no longer a place for them. The fact remains that a cattle dealer will pay a better price for a trained dog than any other stockman. Only proven trial dogs fetch more.

The Sheep-Dealer's Dog

To return to shepherding, sheep dealers often need dogs to load sheep into lorries, drive them into factory buildings and collect those they have bought. All this requires a very firm dog, as he will be strange to each bunch of sheep, and each in turn will look for the chinks in his armour. Again, as with dealers' castle, and suckler cows with calves, the work can be quite dangerous. A dog may be trampled or even suffocated.

Fortunately, the high value of strong working dogs today saves them from some of the rough treatment that used to be meted out to them. The drovers' dogs of long ago had a hard life of it, working to exhaustion point for little food and less praise. True, there have always been those who valued their dogs and treated them well, but before we condemn the others, we should consider what hard lives they themselves led.

THE BORDER COLLIE AS PET AND COMPANION

Working Border Collie? Yes, I think so. If not actually working in the fields, the dog which guards his master's property and person and keeps

Who says Border Collies don't make good pets? Denis Quill and Crannagh Finn.

him company is performing a useful function.

Not all Border Collies make good pets. I shall go into this aspect more thoroughly when dealing with temperament. Certain strains are suitable, others are not. Having chosen a suitable dog, you could find no more faithful companion and, having been bred for obedience, a Border Collie will never be a nuisance unless you spoil him.

My daughter and I once had supper with Dr. Sheila Grew, then editor of *Working Sheepdog News* and author of that very interesting work *Key Dogs of the Border Collie Family*. There were nine adult Border Collies in the house at the time and not once did any of them move. They went to their baskets when told and stayed there.

Border Collies are seldom greedy or noisy. They can be bad-tempered with strangers, but no more so than many another breed. As house dogs, much depends on their upbringing. If they are to be kept in a house with children, it is better if they have been reared with children than introduced to them as adults.

There is an old belief that collies are 'treacherous'. I don't agree. I think this fallacy arises from the fact that Border Collies have a lot more in their heads than most other breeds. In dogs as in horses, or humans come to that, the most intelligent specimens are often the most highly strung and may be ultra-sensitive. There are exceptions, my Ben is one, but the dog which loves everybody is often less brainy than one which is more selective.

The Border Collie is a working breed which needs scope for mental as well as physical exercise. Don't imagine that your dog will pine if he can't gallop miles 'round sheep every day. He'll be all right so long as he has something else to interest him, and a sensible amount of exercise. Consider the working farm dog when there is no work to be done. He will potter about happily with his master all day, and when his master sits down, his dog will sleep peacefully until he is needed again. A great deal of rubbish is talked and written about the physical needs of the Border Collie.

Character and Appearance

BASIC ESSENTIALS

A top-class Border Collie with trial potential must have a number of inborn qualities if he is to be worth training. These are:

A natural cast, or outrun, combined with the instinctive knowledge of how much room to give the sheep.

Enough 'eye' to keep the sheep together and to ensure their respect.

Enough power to face a single sheep and force it to retreat without rushing in, biting viciously.

Enough intelligence to use his own initiative in a crisis.

A sound temperament which will accept correction when necessary and stand training without sulkiness.

A sound constitution.

All these qualities are present at birth. If one of them is lacking in the temperamental or physical make up of the dog, it can't be put there. Ability may be improved by training, and a poor constitution by care and attention, but no trainer can turn a common dog into a stylish one or a coward into a hero.

The Outrun

Some years ago, my husband and I went to buy a dog which was said to be trained. The owner's sheep were in a small paddock, and the dog worked them beautifully, finishing by driving them out of the paddock and away down a hill in fine style.

'You won't see many dogs drive like that,' said the owner, calling his dog back.

'Send him for them again, please,' said John. 'We haven't seen him run out yet.' We never did. The dog, like many others, would only travel in straight lines. Totally useless. A moderate outrun can be improved by training, but there is no substitute for the real thing. Dogs who lack a natural 'cast' tend to cut in close when they get behind their sheep. This startles them and makes a proper 'lift' impossible.

The dog with a good natural outrun usually also has the instinct to keep the proper distance between himself and the sheep when working. As the distance varies according to the number and obstinacy of the sheep, it can't be taught. Teach the dog to keep well away and he will be helpless with stubborn sheep. He must adjust this distance naturally. A dog which does this will not cut corners. He will not make sudden movements or sharp turns unless ordered to do so.

Such a dog is said to be a 'natural worker' or 'good mover' with a 'natural turn'. He is always a pleasure to watch.

Eye

As I have mentioned before, the use of 'eye' is that which distinguishes Border Collies from other working dogs.

At the present time, 'strong eyed' dogs are out of fashion because they

It has taken many generations to breed "eye" into the Border Collie. Glenn, a winner of open trials, shows he has the look.

tend to be 'sticky' and to sit more than they should. In extreme cases, they refuse to get up, seeming to be mesmerised as they hold the gaze of the sheep. Also, they sometimes do not respond readily to 'flanking' commands and are less suited to the light, easily moved sheep so often seen on the trial field.

A working dog must have some 'eye', and he must be born with it. Without it he will be far harder to train, and he will not be able to hold a bunch of sheep up in the open without a lot of running about. A dog with too much 'eye' can be improved by keeping him moving (the hypnotised stare is a curable habit). But if your dog hasn't enough 'eye', there is nothing you can do about it.

I have seen dogs with very little eye winning trials, but not of National or International standard. I was amused by an Irishman's description of two very 'loose eyed' dogs which used to stroll round the trial field in a casual manner. 'They work with their hands in their pockets,' he said. The advantage of a 'loose eyed' dog is that he is flexible and, because he doesn't bunch the sheep tightly, he can shed one off easily. Also he works on his feet. A word of warning. It has taken many generations to breed 'eye' into the Border Collie. Once bred out again it might prove difficult to get back. If you want to train your own dogs, choose a strain with a fair amount of 'eye' or you will make your task much harder for yourself.

Power

I don't altogether like the word 'power' to suggest a dog's authority over stock. It suggests aggressive mastery and domination.

Power is really indefinable. It is a 'way with sheep' to which they respond without question. Sheep have never outgrown their fear of the dog, which is not surprising when you realise that thousands are worried by stray dogs every year. They show this fear by bolting, and when cornered by dogs they will pile up until they suffocate. An untrained sheepdog can wreak havoc.

Obviously a working dog needs to be restrained and guided so as not to upset the sheep, but never underestimate the brains of those same sheep. They are not stupid by any means. They know at once whether a dog will stand up to them, chase them or bite them. They also know when a dog is afraid. They recognise a fresh dog as soon as he appears in the distance and will continue grazing if he hasn't the power to move them.

A good dog trainer must have a way with dogs as a good horseman needs a way with horses and a good teacher with children. 'Authority' is a better word than 'power' for what I mean. Authority in the human race is not called power. We find it in the home, in the classroom, at work. Wherever you go, you will find people who are listened to and respected, and others who are ignored.

This quality can't be defined. It has nothing to do with age, sex or social position. Upbringing can help to establish it but cannot bring it into being. It always asserts itself in a crisis.

Dogs respect this quality in their masters in the same way as sheep respect it in dogs. For those of us who lack it (and I speak from experience) a great deal of patience is necessary. For your dog, there is no substitute for power. You can increase his confidence, and that is the best you can hope to do.

Intelligence

Intelligence isn't peculiar to the Border Collie. They are wonderfully clever as a rule, but have a different type of intelligence from some other breeds, as theirs is bound up to a great degree with instinct.

There is a tendency among Border Collie enthusiasts to class them all as being 'almost human'. This is not true. The work we value them for is what we cannot do ourselves, although some of our human ways 'rub off' on our dogs, especially when they live in our houses. They are not like us and their thought processes are entirely different.

Consider the dog's allegiance to his master. He will leave another dog to die without a backward glance, to go with his master. A bitch will leave

Crannagh Ben, a grand stud dog.

her puppies and follow him, or allow him to take them away and drown them without bearing him any malice afterwards.

Canine brains are *different*. So are canine emotions. That is not to say that there aren't intelligent dogs and stupid ones. There are, and a puppy with a low I.Q. will grow into a dog with a talent for being in the wrong place.

Some owners love their stupid dogs dearly and make all sorts of excuses for them. Even when they bite postmen and welcome burglars they can do no wrong. At work, making excuses is no help, and a fool will remain a fool all his life.

Temperament

There is a type of Border Collie whose work is his life. He thinks of nothing else. Even the instinct to survive is second to his desire to work.

A dog of this sort is the outcome of deliberate breeding of certain dedicated strains. He does not make a good pet. He is not what you might call a 'nice' dog. His master exists to him only as the agent by which he carries out his vocation, namely, working stock. Such a dog will respect his master, even love him in his own strange way, but work is his sole purpose in life. He will ignore danger, hunger, his master's anger, bitches in season. As long as there is work to be done, he will carry on until he drops.

This type of dog is not an easy character to deal with. He becomes frustrated and unhappy when there is no work for him to do. He is likely, if allowed to run loose, to turn to sheep-worrying; an extension of what he regards as 'work'. It is the height of cruelty to allow such a dog to go to a non-working home. Better by far to have him destroyed.

Some of the very best working dogs belong to this category. Unfortunately it takes an unusually capable handler to bring out the best in them. They are often misunderstood and mishandled because their one-track minds and lack of interest in human companionship is 'undoglike'.

The majority of Border Collies retains the devotion to man that stems from dogs' dependence on man. Sometimes the devotion is sadly misplaced, but the dog's instinct tells him that his survival rests with man rather than with his own kind.

The average handler prefers the happy affectionate dog who puts master first and work second. He is easier to understand and to train.

Over dedication to work in Border Collies comes from breeding for performance alone without regard to temperament.

The most serious fault in Border Collie temperament is nervousness. There is only a hairline between sensitivity and nervousness. A top class working sheepdog is like a delicately tuned machine. He has to be sensitive if he is to obey a handler half a mile away. Such a dog requires careful training and can easily be spoiled.

Breeding from two extremely sensitive dogs because they happen to be marvellous workers can be a mistake. The resulting dog may be born shy. This type of dog is never normal and becomes worse with age. It refuses to be caught, shiver and cower, and likes to hide in the dark.

This dog possess a highly developed working instinct, and often rounds up stock if allowed to run loose, but its fear of humans makes it impossible to train. It is of no use to anybody and there is no cure. Dogs that fear humans but behave normally with other dogs are not past praying for. They may react to being isolated from other dogs and treated with the greatest kindness. Generally speaking, however, a dog born shy is incurable and will merely make neighbours suspect that you beat him.

There is no doubt that shyness is hereditary, and is a condition which will continue to crop up as long as shy dogs are used for breeding. Some borderline cases do very well for clever handlers, and they can hardly be blamed for breeding from them. It is unusual to see a whole litter of shy puppies. Often there is just one. Even one is a sign that there is nervousness in that particular strain.

The sensitive type is most likely to become a 'one-man dog.' While it is gratifying for the owner when his dog won't go a yard for anyone else, it is a mixed blessing on a farm.

After shyness, I consider sulkiness the most serious fault of the Border Collie temperament. We are talking about working dogs, and if a dog is to work, however brilliant his intelligence, he must be trained and his instincts encouraged or curbed as necessary.

A shy dog simply won't bear training. A mild case may genuinely want to do right, but won't stand any correction, even the gentlest reproof. He will be made so miserable by his master's annoyance that he will either go home or lie down and refuse to work again. At all costs he won't risk doing wrong. He feels safer doing nothing at all.

At the other extreme comes the dog who thinks he knows it all. He is often one whose training has been left too late. A dog like this is sure he is doing right. If corrected, he is first puzzled, then sulks and gives up.

Tactful handling may cure sulks, but they are as exasperating in dogs as in the human race.

Vicious Border Collies are unusual. Viciousness is usually traceable to bad handling, or it may be a hereditary defect.

Having dealt with the more common faults of temperament, let it be said that most Border Collies, given even the most rudimentary training and care, have wonderful temperaments. They are gentle and clever, happy and honest. They have a sense of responsibility which often puts their owners to shame. A good Border Collie is a sweet-natured and uncritical companion, prepared to serve you faithfully and well until he dies.

APPEARANCE

'It doesn't matter what he looks like as long as he'll work.' This is the point of view that has resulted in the wide variations in appearance of the Border Collie.

There is now a breed standard which purports to take due account of

This puppy's watchful look is typical of the dedicated worker. Breeding from two animals like this may produce shy puppies.

the fact that the Border is a working breed. I view this with some suspicion as the same claims have been made for the breed standard of the Rough Collie.

I propose to go over the points of the breed from a working point of view, bearing in mind that there are different types of work and the same physical type simply isn't suitable for all of them. One thing all Border Collies should have in common is soundness. Colour, size and coat are matters for the individual, but soundness of constitution is a necessity.

The Head

To my mind, the dog's expression is more important than the shape of his head. His expression is the surest guide to his personality. He should look straight at you when you speak to him, squarely and honestly. Mistrust the dog who squints sideways at you, and the one with a sulky or frightened expression. I have known a few dogs who had a wild, half-crazy stare in their eyes. Their work matched their looks. I don't care for a 'bitchy' head on a dog, or a 'doggy' head on a bitch. A dog especially should be unmistakeably a dog.

Ears may be pricked, bent over or low set. The last mentioned are not admired as they may have something to do with gundog influence. I have never found them of any harm. Pricked ears may be deceptive, and they give a dog a bright, alert look. We once bought a half-grown puppy with big pricked ears. When his breeder asked my husband how the young dog was moving round sheep, he replied, 'like a very old man going shopping'. This was an exact description of Moss.

'The bigger the head the greater the brain,' says an old handbook on gundogs. I don't agree. Most of us like to see plenty of width in a working

A dog's head should indicate its sex. Sam is obviously a dog. Bess, equally clearly, is a bitch.

dog's skull, but actual size of head is no guide to brain power. A snipey nose isn't attractive, and an overshot or undershot jaw is a serious fault.

Many people look for a black nose and mouth-roof as a sign of pure ancestry. This is not a reliable test. Plenty of mongrels would pass, while dogs with faultless breeding quite often have some pink on the nose, which usually goes with a pink or mottled mouth-roof.

Head shapes differ according to the strain. The classic type is wedge-shaped with a pronounced stop, but foxy types are common, as well as strong-jawed pointer types with domed skulls. Some of our best cattle dogs have had heads of this last type.

Eyes should be brown, although one or even both eyes being blue is fairly common. The standard allows them only in the blue merle. This would eliminate many wonderful working dogs straightaway.

One usually reliable authority states, 'A dog with light-coloured eyes is never any good.' This sounds as if it might be correct, until one

The classic display of a wedge-shaped head. A properly looked-after Border Collie will usually remain free of health problems.

remembers the large and growing number of brown and red Border Collies on farms and on the trial field. Some of these dogs are every bit as good as their more conventionally coloured relations and they include top class competition winners. Their eyes are usually light brown or yellowish. Sometimes they are green and glassy. These yellowish and greenish eyes are not attractive and they seem to have no depth. Perhaps that is why they are unpopular. Slate grey dog's eyes are often grey too, just a bit paler than their coats.

Very dark brown eyes often go with a soft temperament, although they look appealing. No particular colour is associated with defective sight.

Conformation of the Body

A Border Collie works with his head low, and apart from being unsightly, a short neck spoils his balance. A well-laid-back shoulder makes for speed and reduces the jar on the dog's legs when he stops or when the ground is hard. A broad chest and short legs mean a slow dog. There should be sufficient depth and girth to allow plenty of lung and heart room.

The dog's back should be long enough to ensure smooth action and balance when working at speed, loins should be strong, and length from hip to hock is essential for pace and stamina. A working dog should never look clumsy. His lines should be graceful and should indicate activity. His tail should be set on fairly low and carried low when working.

A tail carried high or crooked is not liked. A dog which is scared or overfaced when working will throw his tail in the air. It can be forgiven in a puppy, but in an adult is a sign of weakness.

Some handlers admire the straight hanging or 'dead' tail, others prefer the tail curled up at the end like the handle of a walking stick. This type, associated with the descendants of Wiston Cap, is becoming the more common of the two, for some reason, in smooth-coated dogs.

A dog's action should be straight, level and low. Border Collies tend to go close behind, but should not be 'cow hocked' with the paws turned out, as this type of limb is not hardwearing.

The Coat

A handsome Border Collie in the full beauty of his winter coat, brushed till it shines with health and cleanliness, is a sight for sore eyes. A woolly puppy like a little bundle of soft fluff will melt the hardest heart.

This book is meant to be a practical guide for the owners of working dogs, and unless you are prepared to spend some time caring for your dog's coat, the woolly type is best avoided.

Strictly speaking, Border Collies should never be woolly, no matter how long the coat. The hair should be straight and silky, with a dense undercoat.

A healthy Border Collie looks confident and happy. Crannagh Ben.

There are other disadvantages of a shaggy working dog as well as the necessity of grooming. He will collect mud or snow on his belly and legs and between his pads. He will smell when he gets wet, he is more subject than his smoother relations to ear canker and skin trouble, his thick coat provides good cover for fleas, and he must be cleaned up after work if he rides in your car or comes into your house. When he is casting his coat, he does it front end first, and goes through a very unsightly stage when his back end is rough and his front end smooth. Some dogs have to be clipped under the tail like sheep to keep them clean.

I like a medium-smooth dog best. This sort has a close dense coat and a little feather on the tail and sometimes the forelegs. I speak from a practical rather than an aesthetic point of view, but I also admire the type.

'Bare-skinned' Border Collies are much more common than they used to be. Their coats can be as fine as a greyhounds, and they are usually of fairly slender build. These dogs are not adequately protected against

Glenn demonstrates the old slate or blue grey, a recessive colour.

weather and rough going through bushes and hedges.

I don't know if it is a generally accepted fact, but fine-coated dogs often seem to be the ultra-sensitive type—thin skin appearing to go with fine feelings! I don't think smooth dogs lack for courage—anything but. In fact some of our bravest dogs have been smooth. I do think, however, that rough coated dogs come from a strain which is easier for the beginner to handle. The desired type of coat can easily be established by breeding.

The traditional colour of the Border Collie is black and white. Mainly black is preferred, with typically a white stripe down the face, white collar and breast, white or black and white legs and black tail with a white tip. I suppose about half the puppies of working strains registered have approximately this colour distribution. Nobody really knows how it came about in the first place. It shows up well and is nice to look at.

Character and Appearance *45*

Tri-colours (black, white and tan) are becoming increasingly common, and other variations on the black and white theme are found, from black all over to white all over. Various shades of brown, from russet to liver, are met with, and greys, blue merles and red merles are increasingly popular.

The true blue merle comes from the old name 'blue marled' or marbled. The blue colour is splashed with black markings, while the legs are tan and the usual white markings may be present. A blue merle must have one blue merle parent.

The colour should not be confused with the slate or blue-grey which is a recessive colour found in some strains, probably tracing back to the old Bearded Collies of the early part of the century.

A probable legacy from gundog ancestry is the mottling often found on legs and faces. Some dogs are mottled all over.

There is a popular idea that sheep are upset by a brown dog, thinking he is a fox, also that they won't move for a white dog, having no fear of a dog of their own colour. My own experience is that once the sheep get to know the dog (it takes about three minutes), it doesn't matter a bit what colour he is. The odd-coloured trial dog is at a disadvantage because he is always working strange sheep, but at home it makes no difference at all.

Black and black and tan dogs without white markings are a nuisance because it's hard to see where they've got to, otherwise there is nothing against them.

With Crannagh Ben's help, the tri-colour Border Collie is becoming more popular.

Dale excels in brains and beauty, as all proper Collies should.

For hundreds of years, working Collies have been bred for brains before beauty. A maxim of one great handler was 'Brains not Beauty'. I don't agree with this. Why keep an ugly dog instead of a handsome one?

A Border Collie working stock is good to watch as well as useful. No one is going to give away a good worker because he is a funny colour, but one might as well, given the choice, keep a handsome dog and breed for performance and looks combined.

When I started breeding Border Collies, I often had to take less money for a puppy because he was badly marked. As often as not, they turned out to be the best workers in the litter. This seemed to prove that 'handsome is as handsome does,' and I expected that funny-coloured puppies would become easier to sell. They didn't, although all were going to working homes. I suppose the suspicion lurks at the back of the buyer's mind that he may be buying a mongrel.

You couldn't find a better all-round Border Collie than my white and black Mac, but in a litter of pups by him, the ones which have inherited his colour are always left until last. All this would seem to prove that we are slaves to convention and prepared to prove it with hard cash!

Buying a Working Border Collie

BUYING A PUP

I suppose the phrase 'being sold a pup' has the same sort of origin as another saying 'buying a pig in a poke'. You don't really know what you are getting. The risks of being landed with a non-worker are not too great if the litter is well bred, but the occasional dud can be found in any breed.

Greyhounds and foxhounds are breeds which come to mind which have been closely purpose bred for generations. There are 'non starters' among both, and they can't be recognised in puppyhood.

The newcomer to working Border Collies is as often motivated by watching television as by trying to farm without them. Regular watchers of *One Man and His Dog* might be forgiven for thinking that all sensible shepherds and stock farmers stroll about, enjoying the beauties of nature, while the work is done by a couple of clever Border Collies. The farmer opens the gates and milks the cows: the dogs do the rest.

This happy state of affairs is seldom the case. It's not unusual for harassed farmers and their bitterly complaining families to spend hours trying to round up sheep in the worst weather the climate can provide. The dog, if they own one, has to be tied up out of the way in case he upsets things. Even then, his frantic barking may turn the sheep back just as they reach the gateway.

If you belong to this category, a visit to a sheepdog trial may decide you to buy a dog. 'What sort of dog?' you ask. A trained Border Collie is the probable reply.

To someone who is already farming, has a fair number of sheep and not the best of fencing, a trained dog is certainly the answer. You have a picture in your mind of what you want. A dog trained to work in any conditions, sensitive to your slightest whim, but impervious to stickwaving and blasphemy from others; good tempered with toddlers, ferocious with intruders—the perfect working dog.

The trouble is that, in the unlikely event of your finding such a dog, he wouldn't be for sale. Top-class trained dogs have claimed top prices at auction without any trial form, but many a dog couldn't be bought at any money because his owner simply wouldn't know where to replace him. I'm talking about dogs over two years old; young ones are easier to come by.

The puppy will cost perhaps a tenth of the price of a trained dog, and often two novices will learn quite happily together. The experts may turn up their noses at you, but as long as you and your dog achieve the desired results, you shouldn't let it bother you.

I will deal first with the choosing of a young puppy, say between six and eight weeks old. This, I think, is the best age for the novice handler to buy. A puppy which has had no training, and has formed no habits, good or bad, will transfer his affection from his mother to his master, and look to him for guidance. You and the growing puppy will learn to understand one another's ways before he is old enough to train for farm work. You will be the one to teach him the early lessons which he will remember all his life. True, you will have some time to wait before the dog is of any practical use to you, but it could be time well spent.

It might seem fairly easy to choose a working Border Collie puppy. Study the advertisements in the farming newspapers and magazines answer one for a litter not too far away, go to the farm and select the biggest pup. You might be right, at that. You might also win the pools, or pick the Derby winner with a pin.

Strive for an even litter. You should breed them as good as you can and rear them as well as you can.

When I first decided to keep some good breeding bitches, I was limited in funds and ignorant of the best breeds available to me. I therefore proposed to buy several well-bred bitch puppies and keep the best. The experiment was a failure. Not one of the six puppies I bought that year, all from different litters, was better than average. Two were useless, two moderate, one quite good. Number six, by far the best, choked on a bone and died (on Christmas day, I remember). That may well have been a blessing in disguise, as some of her breed later went blind. Very likely they suffered from PRA, a hereditary form of blindness about which I was totally ignorant at the time.

Before trying again, I did a good deal of homework, ending with the purchase of three more bitch puppies. One was nothing much, but the other two were outstanding farm dogs, and founded families which are still flourishing. Perhaps I can save you some of that homework which was both boring and time-consuming.

First of all, what do you expect from your dog? Is he going to work sheep, cattle or both?

Let's deal with the cattle dog first. Personally, I think that a dog destined to work strong cattle is best bought as an adult when you can see what he's made of. If you really prefer to buy a pup, you must look for physical development and a bold approach as well as a good breeding background.

Some stud dogs are particularly noted for siring good cattle dogs. You could make enquiries from cattle-dealers, and owners of known cattle dogs. Go for a litter whose parents are both known to be good with cattle, choose a big, bold puppy, and hope for the best.

Breeding isn't always a reliable guide to buying a working cattle dog at puppy stage but it's the only guide you have, so pay attention to it.

Choosing a puppy to work sheep, or cows and quiet cattle is easier, as trial winning parents are more of a guide here. In any case, it's a good idea to look into the breeder's record as well! Successful established breeders don't usually need to take up inches of space in the advertising columns with particulars of the ancestry of the litter. Such particulars aren't always helpful, and may be downright misleading. While on this thorny subject, I might add that I don't recommend buying unseen, unless you are familiar with the breeder as well as the breed. Fetch the puppy yourself, and go early so as to have a good choice. Then you will have no cause for complaint.

Breeding is important, but don't let it blind you to the importance of physical development and temperament. This is why it is preferable to see the puppies before you commit yourself. It's possible to tell quite a lot about a puppy's nature at an early age.

There are plenty of well-reared puppies about, so never let sentiment trap you into buying a weakling. You will hear stories about the runt of the litter winning the International, but generally speaking they don't. Often they are carried off by infections and chills. You want a dog to save labour. That darling little bow-legged pot-bellied puppy will give you extra work.

How then to pick a good worker? There are no hard and fast rules, which is probably as well, or who would buy the others? More than likely

Choose a pup that appeals to you. A long-term relationship is easier with one you are attracted to.

there will be one puppy which appeals to you more than the others, although you would be hard put to it to say why. I think this is the one you should buy. Don't ask yourself why you like him best. You do like him, and that's a good reason for buying. He is unlikely to cost more than the others and, if he isn't as good as you hoped, you'll probably make excuses for him and get him to go well for you in the end.

Choose a puppy that is friendly and attractive to look at. You might need to sell him again, and these two factors will stand to him as companion and pet if you have been unlucky and picked a non-worker.

Worse than the badly reared puppy is the nervous one. I've seen a prospective customer rattle a stable door and flap his hands at the six-weeks-old puppies inside to see if they were nervous. Any puppy may be forgiven for keeping out of reach of someone like this, but beware of one that is frightened of his owner. If the owner can't catch him, let him keep him.

In many cases, the sire of the puppies won't be the property of the breeder, but if he is, you may ask to see him working stock. The mother won't be at her best if her puppies are still young. She will be casting her coat and may not look very attractive. You may ask to see her at work but don't expect peak performance.

I don't usually recommend buying funny-coloured puppies, but I will make one important exception. If one of the parents is an outstanding worker and also an odd colour, I would forgive a puppy of the same colour for his looks.

Having chosen your puppy, check his mouth and make sure he is neither undershot nor overshot. This is a fairly common defect in some strains and quite easy to miss at an early age. A puppy bought 'sight unseen' could be returned for this fault, but you can't expect the breeder to take him back if you have spent an afternoon choosing him from half a dozen.

As for price, it isn't always a guide to quality. A known breeder with a good name may charge more for an average litter than an unknown beginner could hope to get. That beginner might own an exceptional bitch. Prices are often higher too in city areas where a percentage of Border Collies are sold for pets, showing and obedience training.

When you collect your puppy, take a large box and plenty of newspapers. Most breeders have enough sense not to feed the puppies before a journey, but not all. Very few will provide a suitable box. If you don't own a travelling kennel, purchase a suitable carrier at your supplier.

This is also the time to arrange for registration, so check that the breeder has taken the puppy's markings and decide on his name. Enquire beforehand whether registration is included in the price.

BUYING AN OLDER PUP

There is nothing against buying an older pup, between the age of eight and sixteen weeks except that the choice is narrower. Most breeders of good working dogs dispose of all they wish to sell early on. Some have a waiting list. Stronger pups are sometimes 'leftovers' which have been bad doers or perhaps had an illness. Also they take rather longer to adapt to new homes.

Of course some breeders keep all their pups until they are about three or four months old, in order to keep the most promising for themselves. If you can find genuine puppies four months old, it will be easier to tell how they will turn out in looks and temperament. If over twelve weeks, ask if they have been vaccinated, and if not, see to it at once.

Older puppies are best if they have been out of doors or at least in open kennels in the daytime, otherwise their mental growth may have suffered. If they have developed any bad habits like car chasing or non-stop barking, they may take some curing. So I stick to my preference for younger puppies.

BUYING A YOUNG DOG

If you decide that you will have too long to wait for your puppy to be useful, the next best bet is a dog starting to work.

He may be a puppy five or six months old, or a backward adult, but there's no point in buying anything past the puppy stage unless it is showing some interest in stock. Mistrust the seller with a 'trained' dog under a year old to sell. You shouldn't buy a dog in this category unless he appeals to you at once as a sensible sort, and one which you would like to work with.

Some young dogs starting to work don't take at all kindly to a change of owners. It is a big thing in a working Border Collie's life when he first finds out his vocation, and a direction for his half-formed instincts. His owner will probably have taken him to stock and perhaps given him some preliminary training.

The half-grown pup, just starting to 'run' and learn some basic commands, is an adolescent with all the problems of adolescence. Add to these a change of home and a new

Crannagh Chris, a healthy, friendly pup, age four months.

owner whom he may not understand, and you are quite likely to find you have bought a crazy, mixed-up dog!

Accordingly, be extra careful how you handle him and allow him plenty of time to get used to you.

When buying a dog just starting to work, ask the owner to allow him to do as he pleases within reason. You don't want to know how many words of command he has learnt so much as how he shapes up to stock, what sort of style he has, and whether he has courage. At this stage, he may be forgiven for flying in, barking, and perhaps grabbing a bit of wool. What you don't want to see is a dog turning 'round in circles with his tail in the air, cutting out a single sheep and hanging on to it, or bolting out of the field. Look out for a natural worker which keeps his eye on the stock and has the instinct to gather.

Don't worry too much about the training the puppy has had. Unless you are familiar with dog training, you can't hope to carry on straightaway where the last owner left off. It is most unwise to turn a new, partly trained dog loose with sheep until you are certain you can control and catch him.

A word here about professional trainers. Supposing you plan to send the young dog away to be trained, first of all find a good trainer and then either ask him to find you a suitable dog, or persuade him to go with you when you buy. Not only will he be able to advise you, he will know whether he would be prepared to train that particular dog. Good trainers won't waste time on unsuitable animals. (If you know each other well, ask him whether, once properly trained, he considers the dog would be suitable for you.) Firm, experienced handling can work wonders, but if the dog is basically unsuitable for your requirements and ability, the benefit of expert training will only be temporary.

BUYING A TRAINED DOG

Don't imagine that buying a trained dog is mainly a matter of paying for it. Good trained dogs are not often sold except by expert handlers and by those who deal in them. They are neither easy to find nor cheap, and are almost always sold as they stand, so it is possible to make an expensive mistake.

If you haven't bought a Border Collie before, do take an experienced friend to advise you.

Never invest in a trained dog you don't really like, just because he puts up a good show. Your instinct may be sound, and it is easy to be blinded by expert handling of a moderate dog. Don't forget that you are paying and others must not bully you into buying a dog because they would like him for themselves.

As you won't be allowed to take the dog home to try him, make sure of getting as full a trial as possible before you buy. Ask to see him working with the type of stock you need him for. Satisfy yourself that he has enough power, by asking the owner to get him to hold up sheep in a corner and then drive them at him. He should never give way. Neither should he ever turn his back on the stock. When turning, he should always turn *in* towards the stock, never out. This fault is usually confined to underbred dogs.

When you have seen the dog work for his master, ask to see him work unchecked and watch to see how he behaves on his own. This will give you a better idea of your own ability to work him than seeing him perform for a more experienced person. If you have a good dog handler or trainer with you, the owner should not object to his trying the dog,

June illustrates a typical Border Collie in action.

One puppy may appeal to you more than others. These healthy friendly puppies were sired by Crannagh Ben.

although not too much weight can be attached to the way a dog performs for a stranger while his master looks on.

As for the dog's appearance, unless you wish to use him for breeding, it is of secondary importance provided that he is physically suited for the work you want him to do. Avoid buying a dog in bad condition, or one which seems to tire easily. A thin dog with a bad coat and lifeless appearance may respond quickly to improved feeding and management. On the other hand, he may be a chronic 'bad doer', or have been weakened by some injury or disease.

If the dog is unregistered and has changed hands often, it is difficult to be sure about his age. This is another argument for sticking to registered stock. You can't tell a dog's age by his teeth like a horse's, although their general condition can be a rough guide. Perhaps the dog has been hard worked and is past his prime, or if it is a bitch she may have been bred from too often. If the dog is registered, you should be able to check up on his career.

Border Collies don't spare themselves when they work. For farm work they usually keep improving until three or four years old, and are getting past their best by eight years old. The type and amount of work done makes these figures rather unreliable. Trial dogs often keep improving in performance up to six or seven years old, and Tom Longton's Jess was nine when she won the Supreme International Championship in 1983 at Aberystwyth.

Care and Management

FEEDING THE NEW PUPPY

I will start with the puppy or puppies you have just bought. I hope you have bought two as they will settle down together and continue to be less trouble than one. You will find that one puppy will howl all night and you must harden your heart. By the next day he will have become resigned to his fate. Bring him indoors and comfort him, and he will howl again the following night!

Never buy a puppy without finding out what he has been fed. This is not to say that you must follow slavishly the instructions on a diet sheet providing for five meals a day, reinforced with vitamins and tonics. Neither should you pay any attention to the owner who says (as many do) 'Oh, he'll eat anything. Give him anything that's going.'

What you must avoid is a sudden change of diet. You have bought a working dog and he is not a weakling but a well-grown, robust little character with a good appetite and sturdy frame.

Three meals a day are ample for a six-week-old pup, provided that he has a good appetite. Picky feeders may need four smaller meals. You should aim at reducing the meals to two at eight weeks or so, and continuing to feed twice a day until the dog is adult.

Puppies do very well on brown bread and milk as a basic diet. If you don't keep cows or goats and have to buy milk, I can recommend a milk substitute as a cheaper alternative. Never feed milk powders intended for human use; they are usually made from skimmed milk. There are various milk substitutes intended for puppies which are excellent.

If you need to use much milk substitute, one of the types produced for lambs is economical to use and can be made up according to the directions. Substitutes intended for calves are not suitable for puppies. They are less concentrated and sometimes contain antibiotics. In any case, avoid milk substitutes containing mineral or antibiotic additives. Puppy food should be simple, appetising and nourishing.

If you use fresh milk, don't forget to warm it to blood heat as you would for a baby. I once sold two puppies to a man who kept sheep and had already bought an adult dog. After a few days he rang up and told me the puppies wouldn't drink milk. Mystified, I suggested a substitute, and as his puppies hadn't had any milk for two days, I took some to his house. I then discovered that he was offering the poor little things milk straight from the fridge. Problem solved.

Brown yeast bread mixed with the milk makes a good basic diet. Don't give white bread or sweet cake. If your puppy has been fed mainly on meat, mix some with the bread and gradually reduce the proportion of meat. Scraps of cooked beef or mutton from the table are fine, also chicken and rabbit (make sure it is free from splinters of bone). Don't give tinned meat unless it is especially prepared for puppies, as it will be too rich.

Raw beef is fine, but expensive. Cut it small and mix it with the rest of the food, as puppies love it and bolt it down. Don't give pork or bacon.

Cooked potato and most vegetable leftovers are also useful as a change of diet. Puppies need some vegetable matter; indeed all dogs do.

Many dog owners swear by cod liver oil, and it is certainly useful in winter time. It contains vitamin D, the 'sunshine' vitamin, and all young animals do better in sunny weather. This doesn't mean that exposure to strong sunlight is good for them; they generally prefer the shade. I don't find cod liver oil necessary for 'summer' puppies, and while on the subject I should point out that its shelf life is very short. It should be kept in a dark cool place and once opened, either used up or thrown away.

I am well aware that there are dozens of 'complete diets' for puppies, and I have no doubt they are excellent. They are a useful stand-by if you are busy, or have to travel with your puppy. Generally speaking, however, they are expensive and unnecessary. Your best guide to the suitability of your puppy's diet is his condition.

Is he happy? Does his coat shine? Are his legs straight and sturdy? He should not be over fat, or his body may become too heavy for his legs, causing flat or splayed feet in extreme cases.

Whatever food you use, don't forget to keep a bowl of fresh drinking water filled for him. The puppy won't drink much water as long as he is getting milk, but it must be available. Tinned foods often seem to make dogs of all ages thirsty (although they are usually about 75% moisture) and, of course, puppies drink more in hot weather.

Puppies require more food in proportion to their weight than adults. Like children, they consume a vast amount of energy, so energy giving food, rather than mere bulk is a must as they grow older. Obviously, the feeds grow larger as the puppy grows bigger, but he is also growing more active. Don't be tempted to make up extra bulk with flaked maize or white bread. If you do, you will find your puppy is deficient in vitamins. Giving him vitamin pills is the wrong way to work. These should only be necessary if your puppy has been ill, or was already in need of extra vitamins when you bought him.

Young dogs often eat grass and sometimes muck. This is because of a deficiency in the diet. Most puppies will eat green vegetables cooked and chopped.

As your puppy grows older, he won't need his food chopped and will be more than able to chop it himself! The growing dog in good health usually has a healthy appetite.

Feeding the Adult Dog

There is a bewildering variety of dog foods on the market, all claiming to be 'the best.' Some biscuit is dyed in different colours, giving it a very strange appearance. This must surely be to encourage the dog owner rather than the dog. I suspect that the latter couldn't care less what colour his dinner is as long as it tastes all right, and there is no extra food value in the colouring matter.

It is easy to lay down the law about feeding dogs, and it is also easy to generalise. What does your dog weigh? How much work does he do, and is it demanding or easy? How old is he? Your own common sense and the dog's condition should guide you.

The type of food most favoured by kennel owners is the balanced diet, usually made up in 'nut' or pellet form. Fed as instructed, these diets are mostly excellent. Never forget to read the instructions carefully. Some of these preparations are designed for greyhounds and have high protein and low bulk. They are fine for dogs doing hard work, unsuitable for those leading a sedentary life. Personally, I mix dog food with stale brown bread and a milk substitute mixed half strength. This diet seems to please the dogs and they look well on it. I find the pellets alone tend to cause diarrhea if the dogs are idle, and they can get bored with the taste, which means changing to a different brand.

The 'pellets' contain meat and are not to be confused with the various sorts of biscuit on the market. The latter are supposed to be used in conjunction with tinned meat and are *not* a complete diet in themselves.

Tinned meat for adult dogs comes in bewildering variety. As with much else in life, you tend to get what you pay for, and the best brands come pretty expensive. Your local wholesale butcher or factory may provide you with beef hearts or liver, reasonably priced, also large, meaty beef bones, which will be at least as good and far cheaper.

The meat should be cooked, and never feed meat 'unfit for human consumption'. This may be sold cheaply or even given away, but beware. Knacker's meat comes from animals which have died, or had to be destroyed. It may be perfectly all right; on the other hand the animal may have been diseased, or have been treated with veterinary drugs over a long period. It is far better to feed no meat at all than to use this sort of thing.

A word of warning about feeding meat and bones. When you do this, tie your dogs up. The best of friends will fight over bones.

Old dogs need extra care in feeding. Some tend to get fat, and their food should be reduced so as not to increase weight and overtax an aging heart. Their teeth may be no longer able to deal with crusts and biscuits. Soup is a good substitute for bones and you can cut the food smaller. Don't forget that even if his eye teeth have worn down to the gums, he probably has an excellent set of grinders further back!

Some dogs are allergic to certain foods; usually skin trouble is the first sign. This is a matter for the vet. Foods to avoid are highly seasoned leftovers, bacon, raw pork or mutton, and sweet things.

It is always unfair to destroy your dog's teeth by giving him sweets, cake and sugary stuff generally, but expecially so when he is a working Border Collie and those teeth are all he has to protect himself with.

Working dogs should be fed once a day in the evening. Once they have finished growing, a second meal is unnecessary. I have already given exceptions to this rule. Don't allow working dogs to grow fat. They should be fit, well muscled and not poor or thin. If they get thin, give them more to eat—it's as simple as that. Fat dogs which have to work may develop heart trouble and have shorter lives, like their fat human counterparts!

Thousands of dogs taken by anxious owners to the vet have no problem other than being overweight. Usually they are pets, but I have seen a fat Border Collie collapse at work, (not my dog, I hasten to add). Quality not quantity is required in feeding, and it must be remembered that flake maize is not a complete diet. So many people have asked me why their dogs don't look well, and it has emerged that they are fed on flake maize (I suspect because it is cheap). If not well scalded and soaked, it may pass through the dog undigested, and a maize diet is deficient in

A Border Collie's life is full of hard work. Feed a balanced diet to keep your dog healthy.

vitamin B. This vitamin (present in fresh meat, liver, eggs, green vegetables and rice) is absolutely essential to health. Its absence can cause pellagra in humans and a painful and dangerous condition know as 'black tongue' in dogs.

Finally, always remove uneaten food before the next meal time comes around. You may have another, greedier dog always ready to deal with leftovers. If not, throw it away. It won't hurt any dog to miss a meal as long as he has water to drink. Provided he shows no symptoms of illness, feed him again as if nothing had happened, but about half the amount. You have probably overfaced him.

Keep eating and drinking bowls clean. A dirty bowl will stop some dogs eating; others won't even notice. Plastic bowls with no seams are easiest to clean, and cheap. Some dogs adore the taste of these and simply eat them, but I like them best for non-plastic eaters. Otherwise I use aluminium or stainless steel cooking pans, again without seams as they are more easily kept clean. Keep the meals appetising and dogs will lick off every particle of food. I have also used galvanised iron, and found that it never looked really clean and always smelt sour after a few hours.

PARASITES (INTERNAL)

I am following the section on feeding with a few words about internal parasites, because no dog can be truly healthy if he has worms, and the symptoms of worms are often mistaken for incorrect feeding.

Your eight-week-old puppy should have been wormed at least twice for roundworms, and you should find out when you buy him when this was last done and what type of tablet was used.

The amount of treatment for worms you have to carry out will depend on the number of dogs you keep. In kennel conditions, regular dosing with a broad-spectrum drug is wise. Follow the instructions carefully when dosing by weight, and keep a record of doses given. If you keep only one or two dogs, worming is seldom necessary. Signs that it is needed include eating filth, poor coat, ravenous appetite and scraping the hindquarters along the ground to relieve itching.

If you use a liquid wormer, the barrel of a disposable hypodermic syringe is more convenient than a spoon. Tablets may be pressed into a lump of cooked fat or cheese.

Border Collies whose work is with sheep should be dosed for tapeworm about twice a year if necessary. Tapeworm segments are easily seen in the faeces or sticking to the dog's hair. They used to be difficult to eliminate completely, but modern drugs get rid of them without starving or purging. If you also own the sheep you will no doubt see that they too are regularly dosed, which is just as important, as the tapeworm needs both dog and sheep to complete its life cycle.

The hydatid disease in dogs caused by the tapeworm completing its life cycle from sheep to dog to sheep is also dangerous to humans. It is said to be confined in the U.K. to the Isle of Skye and some parts of Wales.

In New Zealand, where the disease is a major problem, the government allocates a large sum every year to its control. For the sheepdog owner in these islands, the risk is extremely small: however, if there is the slightest risk, it can be dealt with by seeing that the dog never eats raw mutton and by precautionary dosing.

Some pet dog owners seem to have a phobia about worms and constantly dose dogs that are kept indoors and fed exclusively on tinned food and biscuits. This excessive use of drugs is more harmful than the worms themselves. Border Collies working on farms and living on a varied diet which often includes offal, are at far greater risk, whereas their owners are far less likely to take precautions.

There is a tendency among many owners and some vets to put down almost any symptom of illness to worms. If your dog's symptoms do not disappear after dosing, it is a matter for the vet, and you must be able to tell him when your dog was dosed and with what drug.

Puppies are susceptible to various infestations such as cat fleas. Eliminate potential problems by keeping the bedding clean and free of dirt.

PARASITES (EXTERNAL)

Lice, fleas, ticks, mites . . . my dog doesn't have any of those! It is amazing how many working dogs do. Puppies especially, with their soft fluffy coats and soft skin, can easily become infested. Lice and mites are not easily seen and can do a great deal of harm in very little time. Lice and fleas are associated with dirt and ill health. They will not be found on a clean healthy dog whose bedding is clean. Both can be eliminated by bathing or spraying with a good insectide.

Ticks on the other hand will never attack a rough-coated dirty dog if they can find a clean smooth-coated one. I refer to dog ticks, not the sheep ticks which dogs occasionally pick up in the fields.

I once unwittingly bought a puppy which was infested with dog ticks and it took two years to eradicate them completely from the kennels. They seem to be indestructible. I understand that their eggs will stand freezing and boiling and still hatch. They live, seemingly for ever, in the cracks in old buildings. There are washes for dogs which will rid them of ticks, but most of these are too strong for puppies, so be extra careful that breeding animals are free from them, and kept in separate quarters if you suspect there are ticks about.

HOUSING

Working Border Collies are adaptable creatures—they have to be, as they have so many roles to play. Again, you come up against generalisation. 'Border Collies are scrupulously clean,' I read in an informed article a few years ago. What rubbish! Some are cleaner than others. Some don't need to be house-trained and never have a hair out of place; others are almost untrainable, and never miss the opportunity to roll in any evil-smelling remains they can find. These two extremes seem to stem from the natures of individual dogs, rather than the way they are treated.

If your puppy is going to live in the house, bring him indoors as young as possible and provide him from the start with his own sleeping place.

A practical kennel and run for working Border Collies.

When he is adult he will appreciate a dog basket, but will cheerfully make do with an old blanket. The solitary puppy needs a place to get inside, out of sight. Whether he is in a room or a stable, he should be provided either with a portable kennel, a suitable box, or simplest of all, a piece of wood such as an old shutter laid against the wall so that he can get behind it and propped up with a brick or weight. His instinct tells him that it is unwise to sleep in the open.

The ideal housing for a puppy or young dog is a sleeping kennel with a run in front, so that he can see what goes on without being free to get into mischief. Working Border Collies have alert minds and their interest should be stimulated in the sights and sounds of the farmyard from an early age.

Some people disapprove of tying a dog up on a chain, but a dog which lives outside is far better off tied up with a view of what is going on than shut up loose in a dark building, however roomy.

A keen restless dog is usually steadied by being tied up when not with his master. Tying a dog up is only cruel when the chain is too short, or the dog is left without exercise. Some collars sold in pet shops are unsuitable for tying a dog up, as the 'D' for the lead is likely to break or pull out with wear. It also keeps a constant tension on one part of the collar. It is better to thread a steel ring onto the collar, and clip the chain to this. The best type of chain is that which has a strong clip and swivel at each end.

Even if your dog is always with you, he should be trained to be tied up without noisy protest. A perfectly trained dog will sit exactly where he is told while you pull a struggling sheep out of a ditch, but those of us whose dogs are less than perfectly trained spend much time and vocal energy shouting—'Sit down! Get back, blast you! Oh for Heavens' sake, go home!' All of which does the dog no good at all. Carry a lead and tie him up when you want him right out of the way.

Dogs should always be either supervised or tied up at feeding time, so that the strongest doesn't get the lion's share.

The most important thing about the dog's sleeping quarters is that the ground should be dry. Clean straw on a dry floor, or a raised wooden bench if you prefer. The building should not be draughty, but Border Collies are more sensitive to heat than cold, and chilliness is better than stuffiness, provided it isn't damp and draughty. Dogs, like their owners, can get rheumatism in damp houses.

EXERCISE
An article about sheepdogs I read some time ago stated categorically, 'The best and only exercise for a working dog is work'.

We all agree that exercise is important, both for body and mind, and the more highly developed the mind, the more exercise it needs. The trouble with some statements made about working dogs is that writers forget that the dog is supposed to be a helper to the farmer. If we were to follow all the instructions offered, our dogs would make more work for us than they do themselves.

Farm work is a seasonal business. Nowadays most dairy cows and beef cattle are kept in sheds or yards for a large part of the year.

The best training for a working Border Collie is field work. The late John Quarton with Dunedin Sam.

Work with sheep continues more or less all the year 'round, but there are busy times and slack times here too. A well-trained dog is needed for work with pregnant ewes and young lambs—you can't train a young dog on them or you will have trouble. Hundreds of thousands of sheep are fattened in barns or yards, and hundreds of thousands of pounds and dollars are spent on sheep handling lay outs. The makers of some of these claim to 'put the sheepdog out of business.' One very useful aid to labour, especially when dipping, is the 'forcing pen', usually circular, which pushes the sheep into a tighter corner by means of a revolving gate. Guillotine and two-way or three-way gates help to do what has also been considered a dog's work, but the trained dog has his place even here.

The trained working Border Collie is never 'out of business'. He makes himself useful all the year 'round, working in buildings, among lambing ewes, yarded cattle and in fattening units. A good dog doesn't upset the stock. They accept him as they do the farmer, but they move much more readily for the dog.

A young or partly trained dog is just a nuisance at times, and often ends up spending weeks on end without any exercise at all. This is certainly wrong, unkind and bad for the dog. I sometimes have to smile though at what passes for exercise with some busy owners. 'I exercise him every day,' they assure me, and it turns out that the exercise consists of a ten-minute walk on a lead.

A dog would get more exercise by running once 'round a small field. Dogs that live together in pens or runs get as much exercise as they feel they need, just as horses do at grass. Take them out walking by all means, but don't imagine that walking on a lead is a substitute for work. You would have to walk for many hours for your dog to get as much exercise as he would in a morning's work among stock.

The best way to exercise working dogs when there is nothing for them to do is to take them to an empty field and encourage them to run about and play together. Walking helps to get a dog fit for work, but he needs a great deal of it, and you will be fit first!

Exercise for puppies is essential, but fortunately they are always ready to exercise themselves without encouragement.

GROOMING

A dog's coat is a guide to his health. If he is healthy and suitably fed, he will have a good coat. Smooth-and medium-coated Border Collies need little grooming. Brushing is good for the skin and helps to remove dead hairs, otherwise they don't need much attention. I don't think baths are a good idea unless the dog has got thoroughly dirty, as the working dog, out in all weathers, needs the natural oils provided by nature to keep him warm and waterproof. Mud should be allowed to dry and brushed off. Overlong toenails can give trouble. Your vet will trim them if you don't fancy tackling them yourself.

Heavy coats need more attention. They need brushing and combing, especially when the dog is casting his coat. Sometimes the hair gets caked into 'cots' at the base of the ears and on the hind parts. These are best snipped off with scissors. There are clean dogs and dirty dogs. Some seem to groom themselves like cats, others generally look a mess.

Although I seldom bathe an adult dog, bathing is the simplest and most effective way to get a puppy clean. Use a mild pet shampoo if the problem is simply dirt. If the puppy's skin isn't in good condition, or he has fleas, a medicated wash is good.

ACCIDENTS

Accidents may seem out of place in a chapter about care of your working dog. If you take care of him, you might say, an accident is just that. Nothing could have prevented it.

For a good many years now, I have been getting letters from dog lovers who have lost their farm dog due to an 'accident' and are looking for another. I took the trouble to list the causes of the accidents, count them,

The author doesn't believe in bathing working dogs—but Bess does.

and decide how many had been avoidable.

Hardly any of those dogs need have died. The only unavoidable accidents were: dogs actually killed by livestock and dogs run over while doing their job of fetching cows home along the road. In some cases they have been killed by cars when the dogs are at their owners' feet. This book is about educating dogs and their owners, not motorists; so we had better pass on to other causes of untimely deaths.

No farm animal is as accident-prone as the sheepdog, particularly the young dog between six months and a year old. This, of course, is the age when the working dog is beginning to need an outlet for his instinct, and if none is forthcoming he will get into mischief and sometimes danger. There is an obvious parallel with the unemployed youth.

I think present-day owners do take more care of their working Border Collies. Dogs and puppies have become more expensive and the TV programme *One Man and His Dog* has brought home to the novice owner the potential value of the farm dog.

Here are some pointers to protect your dog;

Poison

Don't set poison where your dog can find it. Burn, rather than bury, the bodies of poisoned rats. Most modern poisons are supposed to be harmless to cats and dogs. They may do no harm in small quantities, but anti-coagulants such as Warfarin *are* dangerous. Anything that will kill a rat will kill a dog, provided he gets enough of it.

Don't use dangerous poisons such as strychnine.

Never use weedkiller or sheepdip containers for any other purpose.

Most farm chemicals, if spilt, are unlikely to attract dogs, but they will lick up anti-freeze which is very poisonous.

Follow the directions carefully when you give your dog medicine. Don't guess at the dog's weight—weigh him.

Machinery

Dogs are run over every day, often by their owners. A Border Collie, suddenly spotting some sheep, may stop dead and perhaps lie down. The owner, just behind with his tractor, may not stop in time. Or, unseen by the driver, the dog might be under the tractor box when it was lowered. If you take your dog when you are using the tractor, teach him to ride in the cab at your feet. Another advantage of this is that the dog will get to enjoy it, and will stay happily in the tractor cab when you are doing something like fencing and he isn't required. He can't wander off and get into mischief.

A puppy should never be left loose in the farmyard unless the gate is shut. This sounds axiomatic, but apparently not. Puppies being run over by the postman, backed over by turning cars, and escaping onto busy roads account for more than half the accidents I hear about.

A puppy should have as much freedom as possible when he is growing up, but this doesn't mean he should run wild and take his chance. He may wander onto a neighbour's farm and get shot for chasing sheep.

Choking

Accidents arising from choking are more common than they need be. Don't tie your dog up without checking the length of his chain. Make sure he can't jump out of a window or over a wall and hang himself. It is also dangerous to tie a dog to a gate. One sad case, and a true accident, happened to an excitable young bitch whose owner used to tie her to an apple tree as she was disinclined to stay in the garden when there were sheep nearby. She climbed into the branches, and fell out, breaking her neck with her collar. This was pure bad luck—normal dogs don't climb trees.

Dogs are tied up by careless owners with every sort of cord (to be chewed in half) or chain, often without a swivel so they get tangled up. Surely, if a dog is worth taking home, he is worth a decent collar and chain.

Infections

The last hazard on my list is the most easily avoided. Puppies should be inoculated at twelve weeks old for distemper, leptospirosis, virus hepatitis and parvovirus. Boosters should be given regularly. If you suspect any of these killer diseases, you should ask your vet about earlier protection, and keep your puppy away from other dogs.

Damp rat-infested buildings are a source of jaundice. Distemper and parvovirus can wipe out a kennel. It is penny wise and pound foolish to neglect to protect your dogs against these diseases.

If your dog is ill, call the vet at once. Later may be too late.

The author's Mac wasting no time when work calls.

INSURANCE

Anyone who breeds and sells dogs is likely to hear a good deal of grumbling about the cost of keep. This is an extremely irritating attitude in the case of a working dog which after all is unpaid labour.

The biggest expense a working dog can involve his owner in is a bill for damages. If he bites somebody or worries stock, the bill could be, quite literally, ruinous. Naturally, you will guard against this, but you should protect yourself by insuring against damage done by your dog. This can be done on its own, or included in a farm policy along with such items as damage done by trespassing stock.

When you insure your farm animals against fire and theft, don't forget to include your working dogs. The maximum amount allowed isn't usually nearly high enough to replace a good dog, but he shouldn't be left out.

Valuable Border Collies can be insured individually against accidental death, theft and straying for ten or eleven per cent of the estimated value of the dog per annum. These policies, which require a veterinary examination, also include stud risks. Enquiries should be made from bloodstock insurance firms for this, rather than farm insurers.

Training the Border Collie

Training a working dog is not a matter of forcing your will on him until he obeys you automatically. Not, that is, unless you have the task of retraining one which has been spoiled, or starting on an adult, fully developed dog which has never learned basic manners, and can be controlled only by force.

Whenever possible it is best to avoid a show-down with a young dog. Try to avoid head-on confrontations and the necessity of punishment. Let him learn the habit of obedience. I know that many respected and successful trainers preach the exact opposite. 'Let him do wrong,' they say, 'so that you can correct him and show him the right way.' You must be very sure of your own competence to work like this.

I'll take as an example house-training. Now I realise that most farm dogs are never house-trained at all; I choose the example because it is simple.

Method 1: Keep the puppy indoors until he puddles or messes on the floor, scold him, rub his nose in it and turn him outside.

Method 2: Feed the puppy indoors, and when he has finished eating take him outside in a grassy place. Wait until he relieves himself (almost at once if he is young), praise him and bring him indoors again.

Unless the puppy is stupid or ultra nervous, he won't need more than two or three lessons by method 2 before he asks to be let out after feeding. Surely this is best!

EARLY DAYS

All dogs benefit from some training, whether they belong to a working breed or not. Not only do they benefit by it, they need it and feel the lack of it if it is withheld. If no attempt is made to train a dog, he will go his own way and eventually become untrainable.

Many pet owners' lives are ruled by the whims of their dogs and, while some dogs are too dim-witted or too highly strung to be trainable, others have simply been spoiled. This state of affairs sometimes comes about when the dog owner is lonely and the dog has to be a substitute for a human companion. A dog's life is comparatively short, and Kipling

A trained dog in the background saves time, but the puppy should work on his own. Tess shows how not to do it.

warned against 'giving your heart to a dog to tear'. I think it may be the certainty of parting after a few years which makes some owners spoil their beloved dogs so.

Border Collies with their working instinct have an inborn need for someone to train them into the proper channels. They are bred to obey as well as to use their special gift, and the habit of obedience can be noticed as soon as they open their eyes and start to creep about, between two and three weeks old. They learn from their mothers not to soil the nest where they sleep, not to be rough with her, and definitely not to try sharing her food. It is seldom that a bitch hurts a puppy. She will shake it or snarl at it, occasionally nip. She is always obeyed.

At six or eight weeks, the puppy is taken away from his family and his mother's training ceases. He will miss and need it. Sooner or later he will have to be trained, and sooner is better.

You must train a young puppy kindly and firmly, so as to gain his affection and loyalty. Rough bullying methods will gain obedience too, but obedience without trust will be forgotten if the puppy gets a fright. A bad fright can have a life-long effect on him. Trust must be established between the puppy and the trainer, and if you, the trainer, are going to be on the receiving end of all this—affection, trust, loyalty, respect—you must not let the puppy down by showing that you are unworthy. Patience is the keynote. Never hurry the training. Never over-face the puppy by expecting him to do something beyond him. Set him upon easy tasks and praise his efforts when he does well. Keep lessons short. Ten minutes twice a day will do.

I don't agree with rewarding a working dog with titbits, no matter how young he may be. It tends to take his mind off the job at hand. A dog at work watches the stock, not his handler. Glancing 'round is a fault, so is coming back to heel unasked. There is one exception to this rule of rewarding with food. When your dog doesn't want to go into his kennel and refuses to be caught, it helps if you let him out shortly before a meal. Feed him as soon as you get him inside.

Training the Border Collie *69*

The first thing to teach the puppy is his name. Once he has learned it, try to avoid repeating it constantly. When you are working him later on, you will use his name to attract his attention or to urge him on, rather than to bring him to your side.

Not everyone realises how important it is to start early in the training of a working Border Collie. By neglecting to train him early in basic obedience you are making work for yourself later on.

It's all very well to blame the handler if his new dog won't behave, but if he has been bought as an adult he may have developed half a dozen bad habits which must be cured before serious training can begin.

It is vital to prevent your puppy from acquiring bad habits. Curing habits involves punishment, and if you punish a puppy, you must be certain that he understands why, and that he knows he is doing wrong. For some time I ran an advice column in a farming paper and over half my correspondents wanted cures for young dogs between six and twelve months old that had bad habits. The commonest were:

Going alone to stock as soon as they were loosed
Car chasing
Poultry killing, cat chasing
Non-stop barking
Refusing to be caught
Chasing rabbits and other game
Jumping up and general lack of manners.

All these habits are rooted in boredom and frustrated herding instincts. All could have been prevented and all are difficult to cure, especially the first two. Because of the connection with herding, you may affect your puppy's willingness to work later on if you are severe with him.

Never, if you can possibly help it, allow a bad habit to become established. The best way to prevent trouble is to keep the puppy interested in life. Boredom in dogs, as in humans, leads to mischief. It is wrong to say that puppies shouldn't be handled. I handle mine from an early age, and they gain confidence and familiarity with humans.

By the time they are weaned, the puppies should come crowding up for food without any fear. This will make training easier. Already the puppies will come to you; open the door and walk away—they will follow. Your puppy should come to you without hesitation every time, before you start to train him. Then you can put a light collar on him. Don't attach a lead until he is used to the feel of the collar, and remove the collar after the lesson.

A child can teach the puppy to lead, and in fact a child is often the best trainer for a young puppy. He will turn the lesson into a game, and the puppy will learn discipline without knowing it. Some puppies fight the lead angrily, some are frightened, others accept it as a matter of course. From the first, the puppy should be trained to walk beside or behind, never in front of the handler.

Lead the puppy with a light chain rather than a strap, and if he takes to it quickly, don't overdo it. Too much leading about is habit forming and you mustn't forget that your dog's future training will be done by remote control!

A puppy that fights the lead must be taught to accept it; otherwise you will have a much harder struggle later on. Some of them bite the chain, scream, claw, lie down and generally this is because they haven't been handled enough. The best way to deal with this sort of thing is to tie him up to a rigid object and let him fight it rather than you. Don't on any account go away, and as soon as he stops struggling release him and praise him. Often, the most violent strugglers learn the lesson in just a few minutes. If the puppy resists from fear rather than resentment, you will have to be patient and gentle but persistent.

I am quite aware that there are hundreds of excellent working Border Collies that have never worn a collar, been led or tied up. Those who can

Teach your puppy to sit as soon as it is leading properly. The author's Crannagh Ena.

train their dogs without the aid of a collar and chain can skip this chapter, as they won't agree with it anyway. I want to emphasise what is easy and practical.

After his name, the next important word to teach your puppy is 'no'. Speak it clearly and firmly (don't shout) and be sure you mean it. Put the lead on first, so that you can gently enforce obedience. For instance, if the puppy doesn't respond to 'no!' when he jumps up with muddy paws, he will have to be physically checked. A knee in the chest will stop a grown dog.

'No' is a short simple word. A trained dog, setting off at full speed in the wrong direction, will stop as if shot when his handler shouts 'No' The 'down' or 'stand' command is not a substitute. 'No,' means wrong, and the earlier it is learned the better.

Thus, if the puppy persists in barking, catch him, and say 'no!' angrily, with a slight shake. Next time, the word 'no!' will probably silence him without the shake. Those of my own dogs that bark for no reason have all been bought as adults.

Once your puppy will come with you properly on a lead, you must teach him to sit. Again this mustn't be overdone or taught roughly. Most Border Collies seem to have an instinct to sit at the words 'sit down,' or 'lie down,' or at a single blast on a whistle. Some dogs are taught from the first to stand rather than sit, but you have far more control over a sitting than a standing dog. Nowadays there is a preference for a dog which keeps on his feet all the time when working sheep. The idea is that he is more flexible and responsive if he is standing, but the dog trained to sit is more easily handled by the beginner. Provided the dog has the instinct to work, any reasonable person should be able to train him once he is under control. Control consists of teaching the dog to sit, stay, and come when called.

Once the dog will remain sitting until told to come, he is under control. That is why it is vitally important to teach him this basic lesson.

The six-months-old puppy sets off in pursuit of a car, cat or hen. He knows his name, of course, but shouting 'here, Ben' seldom has any effect, (or 'Ben, come' if you are interested in Obedience training with a capital 'O'). 'No!' may make him stop. 'Sit down' or 'lie down, Ben,' shouted hard, will keep him still until you reach him if he has been properly taught. The beauty of this built-in willingness to sit on command is that, if Ben won't come when he is called, you can sit him down and walk up to him. Don't hurry, or he'll be off. Then clip on his lead and praise him lavishly, no matter what you may be thinking.

To call a young dog off when he is doing wrong, use the working command, 'That'll do!' This is used at the end of a working or training session, to call the dog away from stock. It is equally suitable to call him off if he is getting into mischief. If he starts to come away and hesitates, sit him down again and walk up to him. Never run after him—it is stupid and unproductive and the dog knows as well as you do that he can run faster than you.

'Sit down,' in working dogs, in fact means the same as 'Lie down,' that is, forelegs extended along the ground. If the dog is intended for Obedience competitions, he must learn both commands. He must in any case also learn 'Stay!' If he won't lie right down, press him gently down, and put your foot on his chain. Keep all lessons short. Your dog should lie down, because he knows he will please you by doing so—not for fear of the consequences if he doesn't.

An old Scotsman I used to know, a wonderful trainer of gundogs, had a saying, 'Confidence gained; three parts trained.' It is a very true saying,. The confidence must be mutual. The dog must have confidence in his trainer, equally the trainer must have confidence in the dog.

To return to the 'sit down' command; once learned, it is more useful than a stick when it comes to curing established bad habits. Spoken or shouted if necessary according to how far away the dog is, it may even prevent him attacking another dog or a person, and will stop him chasing all the things he shouldn't chase. Until the young dog is under control you shouldn't attempt to work stock with him.

We come back to the question of overfacing. You must always keep your dog working within his powers. Avoid a clash of wills either with yourself or with the stock. If the young dog isn't under control when he starts work with stock, battles will be unavoidable, and it is essential to keep your temper. Lose the battle, lose your temper, and you may find your young dog is spoiled. He has lost confidence in you, is bewildered, has perhaps been punished without knowing why. He gives up. Too often a young dog is punished for doing what he thinks is right. He hasn't understood his master and gets a beating for trying to please him. Very little of this treatment will stop him working for life.

Some puppies are keen to work at a very early age, and I'm all for letting them have a go with a few quiet sheep in a small enclosed paddock. You must remember though that puppies are easily hurt, and should never be allowed near cattle or ewes with lambs until they are mature enough to deal with them, and stand the risk of being knocked over or kicked.

Experiences in early life leave a deep impression, and, while a mature dog can take a few knocks in his stride, a young one won't forget in a hurry.

If your young dog is half-hearted about work, easily bored, losing interest or playing with another dog, he isn't ready for training to work and you can forget about it for a while. Let him run loose with another dog, and don't attempt to check him. A dog at this stage is unlikely to do any harm, and he will probably get keener with age.

Too much insistence on the dog doing exactly what he is told can destroy his initiative. A farm dog must think for himself, especially when working at a distance. It is possible to drill a dog until he will do nothing without instruction. Some trial dogs work like this and win prizes too. The problems arise when things go wrong at the far end of the course. By the time the handler has given the command, the dog has heard and understood and is ready to carry it out, that command is several seconds out of date.

Most stockmen would agree that it is far better for a dog to do *something*, even if it is the wrong thing, than to await a command while the situation gets out of hand.

We have to assume when training animals that they learn by habit or 'cause and effect', and haven't the power of reason. I'm fairly sure that intelligent working Borders do reason. I have seen instances when a dog has shown what was certainly reasoning power, but I think the ability to reason when it does occur is acquired with age.

COMMANDS

The basic training in obedience which I have described involves a minimum of commands—Sit or Lie down, Come or Here, accompanied by the dog's name—Stay, No.

They are brief, simple words. Any dog can learn a few words. A Border Collie can acquire quite a vocabulary in time. Don't confuse him at first with variations. Always use the same word, and persist until you are obeyed. Don't nag at the dog, and do not make him do the same thing half a dozen times. You will find that once or twice is plenty, if properly done. Any dog should learn this much if he is to be controlled. Life will be much easier for both of you.

The next commands your dog will learn when you introduce him to stock. A 'shishing' noise to send him out, accompanied by the direction 'Come bye' (left) or 'Away to me' or 'Way out' (right). Get up. Walk on. Steady or take time. Get back. That'll do.

You cannot claim that your dog is fully trained until you can rely on him to obey these basic commands. Some people teach different direction commands, such as go right/go left, and come in/get out. I think the time honoured conventional 'come bye' and 'away to me' sound better, and if the dog changes hands he is less likely to be confused. However, this is entirely up to you. It really does not matter what commands you use from a practical point of view as long as you always use the same ones and do not alter them.

If you buy a trained dog and he ignores the commands he is supposed to know, pause before you start blaming the dog, the last owner or yourself. Take the command 'Come Bye!' said by an Englishman, Irishman, Scot and Welshman, all with regional accents. It would take a clever dog to guess that all were saying the same thing. Tone of voice is what the dog goes by, and pitch, as much as sound, so a change from man to woman handler or *vice versa* can also be confusing for him. Time and patience should rectify this.

It is a good thing to be able to use a shepherd's whistle, but not essential for everyday work. A whistle is useful at long distances, but many farmers work dogs all their lives without using one. Personally, I think the main advantage of the whistle is that it may conceal from the dog your true feelings if you are anxious or on the point of losing your temper. Your voice will give you away every time.

Expert handlers need to whistle when using more than one dog at a time, each having his own set of commands, but that need not concern us here. I should mention though that almost all trial handlers use voice as well as whistle—sometimes voice alone with a young dog, especially when he is working close at hand, penning or shedding.

When you buy a new dog he must become accustomed to your voice before you can expect him to obey your commands. Keep them to a minimum whatever they are.

WHEN TO START TRAINING WITH STOCK

A favourite question is 'How old should your dog be when you start to train him for work?' There is no brief answer. 'When he is ready' doesn't help much. You can't train a dog to work sheep until he himself is starting to work. This can be any time between six and twelve months, sometimes older.

The basic training described usually overlaps the training for work. If your dog shows no interest in stock, go easy on the obedience training. You may be overdoing the restraint.

Some puppies start to creep about at a very tender age, rounding up everything that moves. You should resist the urge to get out into the fields with a puppy under six months. Hundreds are spoiled by being expected to do too much too soon.

A puppy rounding up chickens at a few weeks old isn't really

A dog should not fear a stick. Bess holds up a single ewe for Simon Mosse.

working. He is playing at working like a child with a toy tractor. His play is an exact imitation of the real thing, but beware of trying to check or steer him. The herding instinct has to be allowed to develop naturally until the puppy is strong and mature enough to work.

Trying to train an immature puppy to work sheep in the open can result in his chasing instead of gathering because he can't go fast enough to get 'round. He may also get over-excited, bark, bite and generally upset the sheep, making them wild and unmanageable.

A puppy under six months old is not physically capable of doing an adult dog's work. Neither is he mature enough mentally to stand concentrated training. The sheep will know at once that this is only a lad doing a man's work, and will make things as difficult as possible. The puppy will try to master them by aggression, lacking the maturity of mind and concentration which are needed for control of stock. If you persist with training when the puppy isn't physically and mentally mature, the stress can cause the canine equivalent of a nervous breakdown.

This generally means a promising dog ruined for life. A little work can do no harm as long as you attempt only what you know the puppy can do, and you must see that he is never the loser in an argument with a sheep.

Leaving the training of a dog too long can result in his instinct disappearing, or he may become too fond of walking at his master's heels, and lose interest in work.

A dog that seems uninterested in starting to work should be allowed as much freedom as possible. Some never start, some suddenly decide to have a go at two years old or more. Personally, I would be looking for a good non-working home for the dog long before then.

Sometimes a dog will start to 'run' if sent with another, especially if the trouble is lack of confidence or over training in obedience. Other dogs benefit from a change of home and surroundings.

The first sign of working instinct is usually the showing of 'eye.' The dog will start to watch the sheep, head and tail low, in the position associated with the breed. A dog which starts to work late is usually quickly trained, provided that he has had some basic instruction.

STOCK

Introducing Your Border Collie to Sheep

When I say that I would let a puppy 'have a go' with some quiet sheep, I don't mean that he should be allowed to chase them about at will, rather that he should be taken out to see what he would or could do. A working instinct developing early must be encouraged or it may die a natural death. The mistake some puppy owners make is in attempting seriously to train an immature mind in an immature body.

If you have followed the suggestions made earlier, and kept your young dog where he could see the normal farm activities going on, and if you have taken him with you on a lead through sheep, he will not be alarmed, but may not show interest either. There is no point in hurrying things until he is eight or nine months old unless he is obviously longing to start work.

A good way of discovering how the young dog feels about work is to take him to the place where sheep are being shorn or dosed, and are confined in a pen or shed. Keep the lead on, in case he wants to dash in among them.

An immature dog may bark and jump about with his tail over his back, or he may be bored. One which is interested will lower his head and tail and watch the sheep in the enclosure closely. He may walk from side to side or he may lie down, but he will keep his eye on the sheep. A puppy who behaves like this in a yard or shed can be expected to do much the same in the open until the sheep run away. Then he will run after them, and if he can't go fast enough to turn them and hasn't learned to run out, he will simply chase them into the nearest ditch. So don't let him loose among sheep in a field of any size, and never attempt training in a paddock that is badly fenced.

The most helpful instinct of the sheepdog is the wish to gather. This is complemented by the sheep's tendency to flock. Some novice handlers start off by allowing the dog to drive sheep away. This is back to front. You don't want to have to fetch them back yourself, and, although driving comes well after gathering in the training timetable, some dogs love it. Once they get the hang of it, they may not want to go 'round and fetch the sheep back.

The keynote of this part of training is working with the sheep rather than against them. Try to avoid collisions of will and don't, whatever happens, get excited; it's catching.

About twenty sheep in a small paddock will do to start with. Too small a number means keeping the young dog well back and controlling him hard, while too many will soon have him running to and fro instead of following straight behind them.

Always take the young dog to the field on a lead. The habit of rushing ahead once he knows what is coming is extremely difficult to break once it is established.

Expert trainers use an experienced dog to bring the sheep out into the open, and turn them if necessary but I must assume that you have no other dog, so it will help if you get somebody to go ahead and move the sheep if they are in a corner or near a gateway or ditch. This person should stay in the field to help in emergencies. Failing a trained dog, he could take another dog on a lead provided it keeps quiet, but never allow a half trained or disobedient dog to work with your young one.

How not to do it. The young dog may not run out the first time. Note trailing cord.

Fasten a long light cord to your dog's collar, and let him go, but keep hold of the end of the cord. He may rush into the sheep in which case you can check him firmly but not roughly, saying 'No'. The idea at this stage is to get him to settle down and watch the sheep. Once he realises you don't want mutton for dinner, he will probably stand or lie, watching every movement of the sheep. Now leave the cord loose and walk past the sheep, keeping between them and the dog (they are bound to be bunched in a corner by now, but it doesn't matter for the moment). By walking past between dog and sheep you prevent the dog from rushing in again, and he may start to run out to the side instead. If he does this, he is trying to work the sheep, and you can follow him quietly, letting him run to the end of the cord and saying 'lie down' just before he reaches it.

Stop at once if he gets bored. Often a puppy will work really well, then lose interest and sniff the ground or wander off. You can't make him start again, so it's wisest to go home, and try again another time. Ideally you should stop before he loses interest, being content with a little progress at a time.

Once your young dog shows that he wants to go 'round the sheep, you will have to get them out into the open somehow. Failing the helper with another dog, you can take your pupil into the corner, leading him by the long cord, very quietly turning the sheep into the open. Let them settle before you try to gather them.

If you let an untrained dog loose with sheep to do as he likes, he will circle and bunch the sheep, and will probably end by holding them up in a corner. Working with nature all the way, you encourage the dog to circle, but stop him opposite you, behind the sheep. To do this, get as near to the sheep as you can without making them run away. Then stop. Make your dog lie down beside you. Drop the cord and try to send him to the right, keeping between him and the sheep as he sets off and saying 'Away to me,' or 'Way out'. If you want him to go left, keep him on your left as he sets off, and say 'Come bye'.

Sooner or later you should achieve your purpose, and the dog will go 'round the sheep. As he approaches a point opposite you, shout 'sit down' loudly and firmly. He may come right 'round, in which case head him off with the words 'Get back'. If, however, he does as he is told, you are in business. The sheep will move away from him and towards you, and all you have to do is to keep him behind by stopping him. Soon you will be able to walk in front, followed by the sheep, followed by the dog. Everything else he learns is founded on this basic movement, so he must do it properly.

You must always keep the sheep between you and the dog when he is starting work; never allow him to come 'round. This is where the obedience training comes in. As long as you can stop the dog at will, you can keep the sheep between you and him without having to run like a mad thing. Habits are hard to break as already noted. Teach your dog the habit of obedience, and go on from there. The habit of non-obedience is equally hard to deal with, hence the insistence on hastening slowly.

If your dog won't obey you when he is a few yards away, you may be certain he won't in a field full of sheep. This is not the place to give basic lessons.

Never send a young dog far for sheep or into a field with sheep scattered all over it. The first will encourage him to cross over or chase, the second is asking him to bring a group and leave the stragglers. Hold your dog where the sheep can see him, and shout once or twice. This will bring in the outliers before you let him go.

Some young dogs tend to be 'sticky' and settle down behind the sheep, glued to the ground, staring. A dog should never be encouraged to do this. It is worse than habit forming, it is downright addictive. Shout 'Get up,' or 'Walk on,' while moving yourself to right or left. When you move, the dog will normally get up to place himself opposite you again. This moving 'round the sheep opposite the dog must be carried out well away from ditches and corners. You can then teach the dog his direction commands. You move to the right, say. The dog opposite at once moves to *his* right, and you give the right hand command as he does it. Then you can get him to bring the sheep to a corner and hold them up while you stand in the corner. This is the easiest way to end the lesson if the dog is keen and doesn't want to stop.

Keep in touch with your dog. Let him learn to drive along a hedge or tree line.

Walk straight through the flock, get between the dog and the sheep and order him to sit. Then you can put a lead on him and take him home.

Working Stock with a Young Dog

Once the basic gather and fetch are learned, it's possible to move your sheep from field to field with your pupil, and he will enjoy this much more than practicing in one enclosure. Dogs that do too much work in the same small paddock can lose interest because they know they aren't doing anything practical.

There are various ways of encouraging a dog that is slow to go 'round sheep and head them. The best way I know is to hold the dog back and allow the sheep to wander through a gap into the next field. Almost any dog will hurry to head them back. Send him longer distances only by degrees. If you send him too far he is more likely to cross, cut in too soon or stop on his outrun. Always stay near at hand if you think an obstinate old ewe may attack your dog. At best she will encourage him to be savage, at worst she could put him off work altogether. You must be prepared to come to his rescue.

Driving is most easily taught in a lane or along the side of a hedge. Walk with the dog to start with, and again, don't let him go so far that you are out of touch.

Shedding should not be attempted until the dog has mastered every other exercise and been working for some time. Cutting out a sheep and chasing it is a common fault with novice dogs, and you must make him word perfect at holding up sheep in a flock before attempting to shed. When you do, start with a large flock, allow them to spread out, and bring your dog through the middle, then get him to drive the smaller number away. Reduce the number of sheep by degrees.

I am not qualified to write about training Border Collies for sheepdog trials. The work is the same in essence, but as only four or five sheep are used at a time, greater control is needed, and prompt obedience is essential.

There is a tendency among farmers to despise trial dogs as 'no good for farm work'. This is nonsense, but a dog that has been confined to trial work for some time will need time to adjust. The great Mark Hayton, when it was suggested to him that trial dogs were useless on the farm, replied, 'It is like saying that potatoes, carrots and corn which win at shows are not much good for general consumption'.

There is no harm in trialling your dog, provided you do farm work with him as well. If properly trained, he will be more efficient than before. Some dogs, kept for trial work, get 'screwed down' until they won't come close enough to move more than a handful of sheep.

Cattle

Thus far, I have assumed that you are training your Border Collie to work sheep. They are the easiest stock to start on anyway.

If you haven't got any sheep and the dog is intended for cattle only, a bunch of calves are best to start on. Next best are cows which are used to a dog. Whatever it is, work the dog on something that moves freely. You can teach a dog a lot with a dozen calves in a large building or yard.

In order to move cattle, the dog must get right up to them.

Purchase a suitable chain and ring on collar for tying, such as this worn by Crannagh Roy.

A dog must be physically mature and in good health before he can be asked to deal with rough cattle. There is a common idea that a good cattle dog is a rough dog. Far from it, he is cool and calculating with sharp teeth that he seldom needs to use. He nips the heel just above ground level, or the nose of one beast, and the word is passed along. Once cattle are properly upset by a rough dog, they can become unmanageable and a positive danger, jumping gates, breaking down fences, and so on.

A cattle dog that rushes in with a great show of aggression is all too often just a big bully which can be routed by a determined cow.

TRAINING THE OLDER DOG

Should you acquire a dog of more than eighteen months old which is keen to work but untrained, your task will be harder to start with but usually the job will take less time. (Assuming that the dog hasn't been spoilt.)

You will probably need to use a choke chain if he isn't used to being led, and you can be much firmer in enforcing discipline. If he is over-keen, you can leave a long cord trailing from his collar (*not* from a choke chain), which you can grab or step on if other means of stopping him have failed. Most dogs improve fastest around two years old, and it's amazing how suddenly the penny seems to drop and the average dog becomes good, the good dog excellent.

The most successful treatment I know for an over-keen dog is to keep him right away from stock for at least a fortnight. I don't know why this works, but it does. An unenthusiastic performer should be allowed as much freedom as possible.

MAKING THE BEST OF A BAD JOB

Once you have owned and worked a good dog, you will find it hard to adjust to anything less. However, even a moderate performer is far better than no dog at all.

For a start, consider what the dog's trouble is. If it's cowardice, there isn't any point in persevering with him. On the other hand, a keen, hard dog that gets over-excited and won't stop or listen whatever you do simply needs a more experienced trainer. Without bombproof sheep, strongly fenced paddocks and a trained dog to sort out the muddles, it's a long and difficult job dealing with such a dog. An expert trainer will be better equipped to do so, and it's worth paying his fee, as you probably have a good dog in the making.

A lazy dog can alter his ways in a hurry if you work him with another dog. This is partly jealousy, and most dogs work more keenly with another around.

A spoiled dog is best put right back to the beginning and taken step by step through the training you would give a pup. Badly spoiled dogs, having been cured by a good handler, usually revert when they change hands.

The most maddening sort of dog to deal with is the one which is almost useless but not quite. Every now and then he will show flashes of

A powerful dog takes the initiative, and the herd backs off.

Almost all handlers have a preference for one sex over the other. Generally dogs are less complicated than bitches.

brilliance and sometimes he won't work at all. I know no answer to this one except a change of home and handler.

DOG OR BITCH?

When you buy a young dog or puppy to train yourself, it's worth remembering that the average bitch starts work well ahead of her male littermates.

Bitches usually learn faster and forget faster. They are quicker to form an attachment and generally more home loving and faithful.

This might seem to indicate that bitches are easier to train than dogs. I don't think this follows. A quick understanding is a great help, but often goes with a sensitive nature. I'm sure it's easier to put a young bitch off work than a dog.

Some of our bravest and keenest Border Collies have been bitches. Little brown-and-white Jess could fetch sixty suckler cows with their calves, and didn't know the meaning of fear—but easy to train? No. Even in this strong, fast little bitch there was the feminine trait of anxiety to please. She hated to be corrected. A cross word made her miserable, but she was so eager that cross words were unavoidable.

Generally speaking, dogs are less complicated than bitches. They learn more slowly and start later, but the lessons remain. Almost all handlers have a preference either for a dog or a bitch. Generally they prefer the sex of their best or favourite dog, so it's hard to get an unbiased opinion. I have no personal preference and feel unable to offer advice.

Breeding Working Border Collies

THE BITCH

In this chapter, I mean to avoid giving quantities of advice which would apply equally to any breed of dog. You are going to breed dogs for work, not for showing. This doesn't mean that appearance can be forgotten. The conformation of the Border Collie has a purpose, as I have already explained. Nobody would deny that there are some odd-looking Border Collies about doing sterling work, but I would advise anyone setting out to breed Border Collies to go for conformation as well as working background. It is perfectly possible to combine the two, and, while superficial differences are of no account in working dogs, weaknesses of conformation must be avoided because they are just that, weaknesses.

The basic structure of the Border Collie varies little—it is temperament in all its myriad variations that causes trouble as a rule. It is almost incredible that one breed can provide so many shades of temperament when you consider that the dogs are all bred essentially for the same job.

We learn from our mistakes, and I have learned the hard and expensive way how not to go about breeding Border Collies. For the moment, I want to concentrate on the Border Collie brood bitch, and the ways in which she differs from bitches of other breeds.

Too often, writers cheerfully inform us that 'the bitch will come in season at about nine months old, and thereafter every six months'. Presumably until she is past it, or dies.

Border Collie bitches, in my experience, seldom come in season at nine months. If they do, it is more often than not, a 'blind heat', lasting less than a week, and infertile. From eleven to fifteen months is more usual, the average being when she's just over a year old. Quite a few bitches don't 'come around' until they are eighteen months old, and some are even older than that.

I have kept records of my young Border Collie bitches—all bred from genuine strains, not inbred, and well looked after and fed. Less than twenty-five per cent had a normal season at ten months old or less.

Usually (and correctly) breeders are sternly advised not to mate the bitch first time. If she is only nine or ten months old, or with some breeds even less, I would be in full agreement. If she is eighteen months old on the other hand, you may not want to delay until she is at least two years old, and she should be mature enough to breed from. If she had stuck to the rules, this would be her second season, at least! If you do mate your bitch during her first season, you must rest her next time.

Another fact I have noticed is that those whose first season occurs at eighteen months or more tend to have longer and more irregular intervals between heats. Out of seven breeding bitches, I have two which come in heat any old time, but usually about six months, sometimes five or even less. Four come in about every eight months, which I find average for the breed, and the other every ten to eleven months.

A bitch isn't, or shouldn't be, a puppy factory. Try to breed a litter every six months, and she will get her own back by producing fewer puppies at a time, and serve you right!

Border Collies are not usually prolific breeders. Litters averaged just under five in a survey of fifty. Those bitches which breed only once in ten or twelve months tend to have bigger litters, and the number of puppies per litter declines with age. It is also worth mentioning that the interval between seasons is usually greater when the bitch has reared a litter than when she has not been mated, or has not suckled her puppies.

TO BREED OR NOT TO BREED?

A golden rule for the Border Collie owner considering breeding is, 'If in doubt, don't.' Breeding is the slowest and least reliable way of replacing your working dog. Commercial breeding should not even be considered unless your dogs have made a name for themselves either as brilliant farm workers, sheepdog trial winners, or in the obedience ring. A good reputation takes years to build; you need more than just 'a useful bitch.'

Before you consider mating your bitch, make certain that you have a market for several pups. It is possible to find yourself saddled with half a dozen hungry young dogs, and, by the time they are six months old, you will be wishing heartily that you hadn't decided to breed 'just one litter from Nell before she gets too old.'

It is wise to take the pessimistic view. If you have orders for six puppies, it is quite possible that when they are ready to go and you contact your customers, four of them will have found one elsewhere. Remember that you may be left with puppies until they are starting to work and you can sell them on their merits. I should add that although I speak from experience, I haven't been unluckier than anybody else. Many aspiring breeders have told me of similar disappointments.

Young dogs need plenty of nourishing food, attention and exercise. If you aren't prepared to care for them properly, or haven't the time, it would be wiser not to breed any. Your profitable sideline could well turn out to be a real worry as well as an expensive nuisance.

There are several reasons for breeding dogs. One is simply the replacement of a good bitch by her son or daughter. The most popular reason is to make some money. The dedicated breeder is interested in improving the breed and building up an individual strain which will be recognised in future years.

There is also the person whose bitches are mere 'puppy machines', churning out dogs regardless of quality, bought for their prolific strains and good looks, and destroyed as soon as they become uneconomic.

Breeding Border Collies is not a way to get rich quick, so the latter type of breeder seldom bothers with them. Puppies, except those from established showing strains, are cheaper than most breeds. A good healthy puppy, eight weeks old, of registered working stock, may cost only a modest sum. It is also of interest that the more the average farmer buyer expects of his dog in the way of work, the less he often seems willing to pay for it.

I haven't sold many Border Collies as pets—a high percentage are unsuited to the life—but I find that pet owners are usually surprised that the puppies are not more expensive. Farmers, on the other hand, are horrified at the idea of paying the price of a fat lamb for a puppy. Don't misunderstand me, I'm not knocking the farmer; I'm a farmer myself. I think it's a failure to move with the times. I spoke of comparing the price of a puppy with that of a fat lamb. Obviously, this is a rough parallel, but it's a fact that, in the years I've been keeping them, the price of both lamb and puppy has risen similarly. The trouble is that the average farmer buys a dog so seldom that he is out of touch with prices.

BUYING A BITCH FOR BREEDING

Buying an adult bitch for breeding is quite an expensive business, as you may have to do a fair amount of travelling before you find one suitable, and she won't be cheap.

It's best to buy a bitch over two years old which has been successfully tested for P.R.A. and C.E.A. Buy her subject to passing the test if she has not already done so. It is also an advantage if she has bred a litter already, as infertile bitches are more common than you might think.

It goes without saying that your bitch must be a good worker, and don't forget that there is every bit as much demand for cattle and cow dogs as for sheep dogs. A calm, friendly nature is very important, and she should be physically robust and not too small.

For breeding, I would avoid buying a funny-coloured bitch or an odd-shaped one, however competent with stock and well bred she might be.

First impressions count, and your customer may have misgivings when he sees a litter of white puppies with brown spots. He will ask to see the mother, and won't be reassured if she looks as if *her* mother had had an illicit fling with an Irish Setter or a Greyhound.

The average farmer, buying a puppy for work, expects it to be rough- or medium-coated, black and white, perhaps with a little tan. Only when you have established a successful strain of working dogs will your name and reputation sell your puppies for you.

A sound pedigree is worth paying for when it comes to selling the offspring, and here it's worth getting the advice of an expert if you haven't studied the various bloodlines yourself. He will also be able to advise on a suitable stud dog.

A winning dog increases the value of its litter.

A bitch in poor health should not be mated. However, working dogs will not always be as well covered with flesh as you would like when they are earning their living every day. The bitch you buy may not be in anything like peak condition by showing standards, but as long as she is in fit, hard condition, there is no reason why she should not be mated. She should be wormed early in her season prior to mating. Even if she is only slightly below peak condition, she should be given a tonic containing iron. Canovel tablets are also useful additions to the diet, and a dessertspoonful of cooking oil with the food once a day works wonders for a dull coat. None of this (except the worming) is necessary if the bitch is fat and well.

THE STUD DOG

It is best to use a stud dog that is personally known to you or to a knowledgeable friend as a reliable sire as well as good farm worker. If he also wins sheepdog trials or obedience tests, so much the better.

It is well worth travelling a long distance to secure the service of an outstanding dog, but if you do this, make sure that your bitch has been accustomed to travelling in the car. If it is her first long journey or she is a bad traveller, she may be upset and frightened and fail to conceive.

Stud fees vary and are usually rather less than the price of a puppy. Some stud dog owners will accept a puppy as fee, but there is no obligation to do this, so make sure of the position first. Fees are paid at time of service, and you may claim a free return service if the bitch has no pups.

Contrary to what some writers have stated, I consider that Border Collies, compared to many other breeds, are undersexed. This probably stems from the wish of so many dedicated collies to put farm work first.

With most dogs, the urge to reproduce their kind comes a close second to the survival instinct with which, of course, it is linked. The Border Collie puts his work somewhere between the two.

I know of one farmer who took his bitch to a very good cow dog, whose owner was about to send him to fetch the cows at milking time. The owner of the bitch insisted he was in a hurry, so the dog was introduced to her, but showed not the slightest interest and firmly refused to have anything to do with her until he had fetched the cows. He then served her without further delay.

Bitches in heat run in sheepdog trials without apparently giving a thought to the males present, and without noticeably upsetting them. In National trials they used to run at the end of the programme, but this rule has now been revised.

Some stud dogs don't care for an audience of strangers, and if this is the case, the dog's owner may ask you to let him hold your bitch while you keep out of sight. This is reasonable, but you are entitled to see the mating once a 'tie' has taken place.

Some bitches need to be held by two people, or muzzled, although they are 'ready' but the breed is not a vicious one, and this sort of trouble is rare.

I have known a stud dog take a violent dislike to a particular bitch, while being quite infatuated with another. This is very much the case with my Ben, who detested a certain bitch called Lark, while he was touchingly devoted to Tess. Quite different was old Billy, to whom a bitch was a bitch, and welcome any time!

A keen stud dog is not only much easier to use but also more prolific. A slow and indifferent dog is a nuisance at best. Special vitamin extracts and hormone treatments help in extreme cases, but veterinary advice should be sought about this.

Unless your own male dog is something out of the ordinary, you won't breed saleable stock by him. Customers want puppies by a well-known dog whose name is familiar to the average dog owner, either by his trial form or his success as a sire.

BREEDING GOOD WORKING DOGS

You may sell a whole litter locally from your own dog and bitch if your neighbours know they are good ones. In most cases though, you will find it difficult to interest customers from further afield until you and your dogs make a name for yourselves.

I would advise anyone breeding their first litter for sale to forget about winter puppies. Litters born between August and February are harder to sell, more troublesome and expensive for you to keep, and run more risk of illness.

Of course, the bitch rather than you will decree when the litter will be born, but I would consider 'missing' her if she came in season in July, August, September or October, unless I had firm orders for at least four puppies.

Every breeder produces some duds. The best we can do is to keep them to a minimum and work always for improvement. When both parents are good workers and well bred, you could be forgiven for expecting the progeny to be at least as good as the parents. This is far from certain. The two may simply not 'click' or suit one another.

The heat period is normally twenty-one days, of which roughly the tenth to the fourteenth day form the fertile period, counted from the first day of showing blood. Again I must stress that Border Collies are less predictable in their reproductive habits than many other breeds. I have known them 'go off' after three days, and drag on for four weeks or more, being successfully mated at eighteen or even twenty days.

There is a myth that if a bitch is mated at the last possible moment in her season, she will produce a litter composed entirely of dog pups. I have known this to be tried with the predictable result of no puppies at all.

With the sad experience of missed litters through bitches with irregular cycles, I try to get them mated on the eleventh day from the onset of heat, with a further mating on the thirteenth or fourteenth day. If you don't

A well-bred dog carries its head down.

own your stud dog and have to travel so far to one that only one service is practicable, it is best left until the thirteenth day. Five days later, the bitch should be 'tried' to make certain she has gone off, and if not, she should be mated again. The fertile time is judged by the bitch's willingness or otherwise to stand for service.

As for the actual mating, I have read pages of complicated instructions, which tempt one to wonder whether it is some new and difficult activity which is being described. If dogs could read, they would be astonished!

In general, I am in favour of introducing the animals, allowing them to play about for a short time, then holding the bitch as long as necessary, and thereafter allowing nature to take its course.

Only if the bitch tries to bite the dog or to lie down, or persists in dragging him about, need she be held throughout. Generally speaking, unless she is a maiden, this isn't necessary and only occurs when she is barely ready for mating or is starting to go off.

The Border Collie's temperament is more important than the shape of its head.

Neither dog nor bitch should be fed within three or four hours of mating, and when you take your bitch to the dog by car, don't forget to give her a walk and allow her to empty her bladder.

I need hardly add that the bitch must be securely shut up both before and after mating. It is possible for her to conceive to two matings and produce a mixed litter. If the worst occurs, and she gets accidentally mated with an unsuitable dog, she can have an injection within thirty-six hours which will render the mating infertile. The snag about this is that the bitch will appear to embark on another three week's heat, during the whole of which she will be attractive to males. She cannot, however, conceive during this time.

To be sure of breeding at least reasonably good working dogs, some knowledge of genetics is an advantage. You don't have to be a walking Stud Book to take in the basic principles. It is unwise and expensive to rely on chance and luck. I am so often told of the gift puppy working at three months old, the big winner bought for a fiver—it can happen, but these are exceptions. If they weren't, we wouldn't hear about them.

When breeding working Border Collies to be sold as untried puppies, it is of the utmost importance to try to produce a type that the average farmer can handle. For goodness sake, don't try to breed trial winners unless you yourself are interested in trials and anxious to train your own homebred dogs to run in them.

You must breed them as well as you can and rear them as well as you can. DO try to breed the best possible farm dogs. Then those that fall into suitable hands may win competitions. DON'T aim for trial potential when breeding, in the belief that the misfits will do for farm work.

Sheepdog trials and obedience competitions require the same basic obedience training that all farm dogs should receive as puppies. Most trial dogs have done at least some ordinary farm work; some winners are farm dogs first and trial dogs second.

Never get the idea that an average farm dog is something not good enough for competition—a failed trial dog. A trial dog is a top-class farm dog with a suitable temperament and a skilful handler. The rest is useless without the last.

Your ambition should be to produce calm sensible dogs with good herding ability and robust constitutions. Don't get over excited when you see a fast, highly strung dog giving a dashing display in the trial field. Before rushing across to ask the owner about the stud fee, ask yourself some down-to-earth questions: Is that the sort of dog I could work? Could I train a young dog with that type of temperament? Could I think quickly enough to anticipate his behaviour? Could my neighbour, who wants a puppy, manage a dog like that? Unless the answer to all these questions is 'yes,' you would be well advised to use a steadier type of stud dog.

When I say 'steady', I don't mean common. Many dogs of the highest class and most aristocratic breeding have easy natures and cool temperaments. Often the big, heavy, rough-coated dogs seem to be steadier and less nervy than the smooth-coated long-legged type often associated with pricked ears and a narrow head. This aspect plays into the hands of the breeder, as puppies of what is considered the traditional type are certainly more attractive to the average buyer. Having sold both sorts for many years, I have had plenty of opportunities for proving this.

The vital thing to remember is that, no matter what sort of dog you are producing, it should be good of its type and suited to an average handler.

Excitable, highly strung dogs, whose owners can't control them properly, give the working Border Collie a bad name. When breeding working dogs, whether they are Border Collies or not, you must try for uniform merit. One super dog can temporarily make your name as a breeder, but you will soon be forgotten again if you can't produce an even high standard through the years.

By using the most convenient stud dog, regardless of his breeding and his ability to sire sound working stock, you are taking a gamble which may or may not pay off. Possibly he will suit your bitch, and the puppies will be as good as their parents or better, but things don't usually work out so well.

I remember only too well our first litter of Border Collie puppies. The mother was purebred, non registered, a good average farm bitch with a kind nature. The father was outstanding—old Roy whom I have mentioned before. We could be forgiven for expecting a litter of better than average puppies, and I had over twenty enquiries from neighbours who thought likewise. We were disappointed. There were six puppies, and five went to the farm homes which were waiting for them. We kept number six for ourselves—the biggest, handsomest dog pup in the litter.

This dog managed to be savage, timid and plain stupid all at the same time—quite an achievement. We persevered with him for almost two years, but his temper got worse and for the sake of my baby daughter, we decided to have him destroyed. Of the remaining five puppies, three were impossibly nervous, one was reasonably good, though not over bright, and the other died young.

This experiment almost stopped me breeding sheepdogs for good, but the result had been so disastrous that I was curious, and enquired further into the breeding of the parents (about a year too late). I discovered that they were uncle and niece, not an unpopular cross in dog-breeding circles. However, the dog which was sire of one and grandsire of the other was the result of a half-brother/half-sister mating. The dog responsible for the half-brother and sister was a brilliant winner of trials on his day, but well known for being moody and uncertain. He himself was linebred like most of the old timers.

The International Sheep Dog Society issues certificates for all registered Border Collies, stating the names and numbers of both parents. For prospective breeders, this information quite simply isn't enough. A mere handful of stud dogs dominate the breeding scene, and puppies are sent by their breeders to all parts. If you don't find out more of your bitch's pedigree than the names of her parents, you may well make the same mistake as we did, and finish up with worthless animals which have to be destroyed.

It is usual for newcomers to the Border Collie scene to think that little close breeding has taken place among them in the past, so they will be able to work wonders with carefully planned inbreeding. This is a dangerously false idea. When the Border Collie began to evolve as a separate breed from the other collie varieties more than a century ago, close inbreeding was carried out in order to establish working characteristics. It should also be remembered that those early collies mostly belonged to hill farmers and shepherds, whose time was fully occupied and whose means of transport were limited. Many dogs were bred from closely related stock due to lack of choice.

The working Border Collie is (or should be) a sound, hardy dog, capable of great feats of endurance. In the old days, it was often a case of the survival of the fittest. With the growing popularity of the breed as pet and companion, hereditary weaknesses are creeping into the breed. Weaknesses affecting a dog's capacity for working can escape unnoticed and be transmitted.

Serious breeders try to build up a successful strain over the years, keeping only their best bitches, and linebreeding to consolidate the strain. For instance, if you have bred a top-class dog from your best bitch, you might consider mating him with a good bitch by the same sire as his mother. This breeding pattern has been used successfully in the past. Before you take such a step however, you must carefully study the breeding of both dogs, as well as the performance of the dogs themselves, taking all their faults into account. If you don't do this, you may bring dormant failings to the surface. You may also lose the vigour and stamina without which a working dog is worthless.

If the dogs you are breeding seem less robust, more sensitive or smaller than either parent, no matter how stylish their work, you have had a direct warning that it's time to look for an outcross, in order to restore vigour.

The advantages of an outcross are easy to overstress. If the unrelated dog you use isn't at least as good as the strain you are trying to improve, the advantages will be only physical.

Working dog owners often furiously deny the usefulness of inbreeding or linebreeding, and for the novice breeder, it is best avoided. It is perfectly possible to breed sound healthy stock from closely related parents, as the breeders of show champions prove, but the wastage involved isn't often mentioned by those breeders.

This is a subject which must be closely studied if it is to succeed. A pedigree must be more than a list of names, you must know a great deal about the dogs concerned. It is often pointed out that you cannot introduce a quality by linebreeding that is not already there; you can only improve the good and worsen the bad by concentration. Unfortunately, the qualities already there may include all sorts of undesirable traits. Recessive characteristics can crop up after ten generations or more.

Take for example a fairly common defect, the overshot jaw. You would not, I hope, breed from a dog or bitch with this defect. It is undeniable that such dogs have been bred from in the past and their progeny registered. I know of a number of cases myself. In the resulting litter, some puppies would have overshot jaws, the others, while normal themselves, would carry the defect. The novice breeder might unknowingly mate two carriers, themselves related, with the idea of improving on a good point in the common ancestor; say a good outrun. Result: puppies with marvellous outruns and overshot jaws.

This is an over-simplification designed to show the pitfalls of linebreeding without adequate preparation. There is inbreeding in nature of course where the rule is the 'survival of the fittest', but the wastefulness of nature is well known. Better a vigorous litter of average working dogs than one super-star and perhaps defective or deformed brothers and sisters. Even worse, some defects don't become apparent until the dogs are working and perhaps sold to new homes.

To sum up, start your breeding programme with good animals which have proved they can breed true to type. Use dogs and bitches which have inherited their parents' best points. Never, never breed from a useless bitch in order to save something from the wreck. Not, that is, if you want to continue breeding. The only possible excuse for breeding from such a bitch would be if her parents were something very special and others of her litter were also very good.

Here I have to plead guilty myself. It seemed reasonable to expect the litter sister of an International winner to breed well by a champion of champions, even though she herself was a moderate worker. Mine was handsome and good natured. Her parents were outstanding. From three litters, all by the best sires available, she bred only one daughter worthy to carry on her line. She bred some very inferior workers and some dogs too nervous to be of any use. Cancer of the stomach claimed her while still quite young. This was a disappointing attempt to upgrade our stock through the use of illustrious names rather than personal experience of each dog's character. This bitch produced some very inferior dogs, far below the standard of what we were breeding when we got her.

REGISTRATION

Anyone considering breeding working Border Collies would be well advised to write first to the International Sheep Dog Society for particulars of membership. In order to register puppies, the owners of both stud dog and bitch must be members of the Society. You can join on a yearly basis or become a life member. There are various benefits for members, including free admission to national trials. The Society issues an informative newsletter every June and December, and stocks books and souvenirs.

Stud Books are issued every year and, although expensive, are a mine of information. Buy the current issue, and you will find particulars of every dog registered in the preceding year—over six thousand on average. Say you have bought a good young registered dog, you can look up the addresses of the owners of the rest of the litter. The books are invaluable to me, and a complete set is a collector's item.

Make sure when you buy your brood bitch that her registration is in order and that she has been transferred by her previous owner into your name. When the bitch is mated, the owner of the stud dog will need particulars, so you should take her registration certificate with you. He will then fill in a mating card with the details and forward it to the Society within twenty-one days. In due course, usually about four weeks, you will receive a folder containing diagrams on which to fill in the puppies' markings, while on the back are the Stud Book rules.

Registration fees depend on whether or not the parents have been tested for PRA, and CEA. The fee when both parents are tested is nominal per puppy, but when either only one or neither parent is tested, the fee is more than three times the amount. In cases when one or both of the parents is under two years old, the minimum age for eye-testing, the fee is about half this per pup.

These cases are granted a green 'C' card, which is a temporary certificate and is subject to cancellation if, on attaining two years, either parent should fail the eye test. For this reason, it is unwise to breed puppies from untested parents, and a dog of two years old or more may be bought subject to passing the test if he is intended for breeding.

If you mean to breed many working Border Collies, you would be well advised to register a personal prefix or suffix. The fee for this is money well spent, and your dogs will be instantly recognisable as being of your breed for the rest of their lives, no matter how often they may change hands.

Quite apart from the fact that registered dogs and puppies are more saleable than the others, if you don't register, it will be difficult for you to keep accurate records, and this you must do. If you start with unregistered stock and they turn out well, you will find it an expensive and troublesome business getting your dogs registered on merit. Your own records of breeding will not be accepted officially, and your breeding programme will be handicapped from the outset.

DEVELOPING YOUR OWN STRAIN

In the beginning there is bound to be some guesswork about the results of your breeding patterns. You may have to experiment by using two or more stud dogs before you finally find one to suit the good bitch you started with. I have talked about the pitfalls of linebreeding, but all Border Collies are more or less related, and if you wish to develop a strain noted for its working qualities, you will have to linebreed up to a point or your dogs won't breed true to type. But these are your own dogs and you have studied them and know their faults as well as their virtues.

Linebreeding to my dog Billy as follows produced dogs with Billy's power and coolness but without his tendency to sulk. This characteristic would be lessened by the presence of the kind, sweet-natured Ben and Moyne, also Billy's best daughter, Tess.

Dunedin Sam	Sire Crannagh Max II	Sire Ben	Sire Mrs. Arthur's Roy
			Dam Thos Loupton's Bess
		Dam Crannagh Dove	Sire Billy
			Dam Moyne
	Dam Crannagh Trim	Sire Billy	Sire Glen
			Dam Lark
		Dam Bess	Sire Lad
			Dam Lassie

Kilkieran Polly	Sire Crannagh Al	Sire Billy	Sire Glen
			Dam Lark
		Dam Crannagh Gael	Sire Templeton's Roy
			Dam Nan
	Dam Crannagh Ash	Sire Ben	Sire Mrs. Arthur's Roy
			Dam Thos Loupton's Bess
		Dam Tess	Sire Billy
			Dam Peg

No. 2 shows the pedigree pattern reversed. I feel that this amount of linebreeding is as close as the breeder of working dogs should go. With this degree of relationship there is little danger unless the key dog has a known defect.

My Ben bred by Thomas Longton from his father's most famous line is an excellent dog in temperament, working ability and looks. He is also a proven sire. Linebreeding to Ben would at first sight seem a good idea. This is where some knowledge of pedigrees comes in.

Ben has three crosses of the great Wiston Cap, so that puppies with two crosses of Ben would have six crosses of Wiston Cap through Ben, and almost certainly others. Wiston Cap had sixteen crosses of the great J.M. Wilson's Cap, 3036, so Ben has forty-eight crosses of Cap through Wiston Cap, and many more besides. The puppies would have ninety-six crosses of Cap through Ben alone! Cap carries, among other things, a factor for brown coats, so one result you could expect would be a high proportion of brown puppies.

What Next?

I had been studying the breeding of thoroughbred horses for many years before I began to take an interest in working Border Collies. When I traced the descent of today's leading dogs, I was forcibly struck by the likeness of breeding patterns between dogs and horses.

Before you protest—'This book is supposed to be about dogs!'—do consider for a moment the rise to supremacy of the British Thoroughbred horse, its gradual decline as foreign influences came in, and what was done to combat that influence.

All thoroughbred horses trace to one of three foundation stallions in direct male line. The Darley Arabian, the Godolphin Arabian and the Byerley Turk. These three sires were used for close inbreeding which would be disastrous if practiced on today's fragile thoroughbreds.

This can be compared to the origins of the Border Collie. Old Hemp, Brown's Spot and Herdman's Tommy were used for close inbreeding in order to consolidate working qualities. A few decades later, the same practice was used with J.M. Wilson's dogs.

To return to the horses; three great sires appeared about two hundred years ago, each descended from one of the earlier three. They were Eclipse, Matchem and Herod. More close breeding ensued until the male line of Eclipse became even more dominant. In the middle of the present century, top racehorses already carried the blood of Eclipse hundreds of times over in their veins.

Then the cry was heard, 'What is wrong with our racehorses?' Unsoundness, ungenerous temperaments and infertility had crept into the breed. Lack of stamina was deplored, as was inability to stand training.

Horse racing is more of an industry than a sport; it can't fairly be compared with sheepdog trialling, and might seem to have no bearing on the breeding of working dogs. But to me, these defects sound horribly familiar.

J.M. Wilson's Cap 3036 was the 'Eclipse' of the sheepdog world. He and a handful of other stars of the trial field have been used indiscriminately at stud by breeders whose sole aim was to sell puppies.

Bloodstock breeders have financial resources far beyond those of most sheepdog fanciers, so it's interesting to see what these rich and knowledgeable men did to counteract the decline in vigour among their horses when they found that their best was no longer good enough.

Did they introduce Arabian blood for stamina, or pony blood for soundness and fertility? The modern thoroughbred derives from both those breeds. No, they introduced fresh blood from abroad into the old structure. It is still the same breed. The influence of Eclipse is still as strong but has descended through different channels. It worked.

The Border Collie is of mixed ancestry, and in the early chapters of this book I mentioned some of the breeds which have influenced the make-up of the dog we know today.

It is not wise to try any fresh 'mixing'. If for example your dogs lack stamina, a crossbred stud dog is most unlikely to improve matters, however good a worker he may be himself. There have been brilliant performers whose ancestry is mixed, but they have not bred true to type—it would have been strange if they had. It takes many generations for the outside element to be absorbed, as it will be eventually. Most of us are in too much of a hurry for that.

In the modern Border Collie, we have a marvellous breed comprising many families or 'breeds within a breed'. You can see registered dogs, solid, easygoing characters, getting on with their work year in, year out. They aren't much like some of the spindly little creatures, afraid of their own shadows, also pedigreed but bred without regard to anything but quick profit. Yet Derby winners have sired hunters, and many an unassuming farm dog can claim an International Champion as his sire. It is up to breeders to choose wisely from the materials at hand.

PREGNANCY
Pregnancy in the bitch lasts approximately sixty-three days or about nine weeks. I have known one to have a normal litter twelve days early, after a car journey had upset her. Another was twelve days late. These two bitches, Nell and Judy, were due on the same day. There was more than three weeks between the litters. Such cases are not normal, and usually you can reckon on not more than three days either way.

A small litter, three puppies or less, is usually carried longer than a bigger one, so if your bitch is unduly heavy you may expect her to be a day or two early. Another bitch of mine produced a single puppy eight days after she was due, just as we had decided that she'd had a phantom pregnancy (not unusual in an older bitch), and was not in whelp at all.

A bitch which was in a good, hard, working condition at the time of mating should not have any problems during pregnancy. If she is working stock you should allow her to carry on with her job until she grows heavy, provided she is not working with rough cattle or ewes with young lambs. This is common sense. A sudden change in routine is pointless and can even be harmful, but you don't want her to be kicked by a bullock or knocked over by a ewe.

Work will keep her muscles toned up and stimulate her appetite. Many a farm bitch carries on as usual until the very day she whelps and is upset if not allowed to work.

The amount of work your pregnant bitch can or should do depends on (a) the type of stock kept; (b) the size of the litter and accordingly the weight and bulk of the bitch; and (c) her health and temperament.

Just as in humans, dogs can have sick pregnancies. My old Tess always did every time, and I've known others. They certainly suffer from morning sickness, eating regularly in the evening but refusing anything earlier. This sickness, which doesn't as a rule involve actual vomiting, usually starts around the fifth week and continues intermittently until about a week before the puppies are due. It is accompanied by an understandable unwillingness to work. More usually, the bitch is normal until a week or ten days before she is due, then goes off her food for a day or two only.

Some bitches are proper old soldiers, and their refusal to work is the first certain sign that they are pregnant. Other early signs of pregnancy are listlessness, and in the case of a first litter, the teats become more noticeable, and pinker than before in colour. Border Collie bitches carry their litters far forward inside the rib cage. This makes it difficult to be sure they are in whelp until three weeks or less before they are due. It is sometimes possible to tell at an early stage, about twenty-one to twenty-eight days after mating, when the puppies may be felt rather like beads on a string well back. This stage soon passes and isn't a very reliable guide.

Many food additives and tonics are on the market for pregnant and lactating bitches, but I don't feel that much pill-popping is necessary if the bitch is fit and well. A tonic containing iron may be given, or a food supplement in tablet form. I think a nourishing diet and sensible exercise are more important.

For the first five weeks, feed as usual unless the bitch starts to lose condition, usually a sign that she is carrying a larger than average litter. During pregnancy it is always best to feed moderate amounts twice daily, as smaller meals are more appetising and less likely to lead to loss of appetite. Change drinking water daily and, should food be left uneaten, take it away.

An occasional meal missed is no harm, but if your bitch stubbornly refuses food, as some do, you should tempt her appetite with something different. A raw meaty bone is seldom left untouched in my experience, and cooked leftovers from the house can make a welcome change of diet.

For the last three weeks, increase the food and give two good meals a day, with a snack midday if the bitch is heavy. An egg beaten in milk is good and can be continued after the puppies are born. I have said in the past 'for the last three weeks, give the bitch as much as she will eat'. Border Collies aren't usually greedy, but there are exceptions. Don't stuff a greedy bitch with food. If she gets over-fat she could have trouble whelping, and she will certainly have an uncomfortable time if the unborn puppies get over-fat.

The working bitch has a big advantage when it comes to whelping, that of fitness. If she is one of those who go on strike during pregnancy, she will tend to get fat and soft surprisingly quickly. Old bitches also often put on more weight than they should. Plenty of exercise is the answer, and *quality* rather than quantity when feeding.

I give all bitches a booster against parvovirus about eighteen to twenty-one days before they are due. This will protect the puppies as long as they are suckling.

If you keep your bitch in a kennel or tied up as a rule, she will need different quarters and she will take a little time to accustom herself to new surroundings. All ours whelp in loose boxes bedded up with oaten straw, and our puppy mortality during the first week of life has been zero for years, so I can recommend this sort of housing wholeheartedly. The stable must be dry, and the door must be kept closed if people are liable to peer in as they go by. In my experience, the working bitch is a sensible creature whose wants are simple and few. They are exactly what you would expect; warm dry bed, and, at the time of whelping, dim light and

Too much of a good thing. June with five-week-old litter by Crannagh Ben.

privacy. I have tried putting a large box in the stable for my bitches, lined with newspapers, but I have never known one which didn't reject it in favour of a nest of straw in a corner. Don't overdo the straw, by the way. A newborn puppy could get lost in it.

WHELPING

The actual whelping, like mating, is a subject which has had whole books written about it. My experience with whelping bitches, although confined to Border Collies, extends to half a dozen different types of mother within this fascinating breed. I find that for the most part, bitches prefer to be left alone to get on with it, are most efficient at coping and sometimes resent interference.

I have only twice known a bitch to have difficulties at the actual birth, and on both occasions the puppies were overdue and very fat. One bitch needed a little help with the first puppy, the other managed herself, but it was a long business and left her exhausted. Any real problems should be dealt with by a vet. Small animals like dogs and cats are difficult for the amateur to handle, and a Caesarean might be necessary.

Try to avoid trouble by taking sensible precautions. Don't mate a light narrow type of bitch to a dog with a big, broad head. Breeding like to like is the natural thing, and usually trouble free.

If yours is not a farm home, substitute any dry shed free from draughts for the stable, and move the bitch into it about ten days before she is due. Make sure that she can't get out. Many bitches have an urge, which must be a legacy from their wild ancestors, to produce in inaccessible places. I take this as proof of their fondness for privacy. If not securely shut in, they may dig a hole in a bank somewhere, or burrow under a building, remaining undiscovered until the cry of a newborn puppy is heard.

She may settle better if you tie her up in her new quarters for a day or two, but never tie her up within a week of the date she is due or when she is suckling puppies. As the time approaches, she will make nests in various places, finally settling on the site she considers most suitable.

Working bitches which are also pets and kept indoors are rather different. They are more likely to want company. I sometimes feel that the owners who claim that all their bitches are miserable without their constant presence when whelping are suffering from delusions. My own favourites, which I have owned longest and which are certainly fond of me, like to have me around as the first pains come. This need of human company continues until the first puppy appears and after that humans are of secondary importance until all the puppies have been born and cleaned up.

You should not disturb the bitch after whelping until she has had a chance to rest and all the puppies have got some colostrum. She won't be hungry but will welcome a drink. Then you should take out the soiled bedding and burn it. I mentioned oaten straw. Failing this, wheaten straw will do at a pinch, but never use barley straw. Newspapers are the next best thing.

Don't allow anyone to look at the puppies even through the door for the first day or two. Try to resist your own urge to find out straightaway the sex of the puppies. Your bitch needs peace and quiet, just as a human mother does.

The Newborn Litter

Very few Border Collie bitches are so woolly that the puppies have difficulty in finding their teats, but it can happen, and if it does, you must clip off some hair. Even then it shouldn't be necessary unless the puppies are weak. Usually the progeny of a young bitch are stronger and more active than those from an older mother.

One problem that sometimes occurs is that there is a gap in the bitch's labour. She might have five puppies within a period of two or three hours, clean them up, rest, and several hours later produce two or three more. These latecomers naturally go short of milk for a time. They generally catch up with the others in the end; a good mother will see to that.

I was once made to feel very foolish when my bitch Rose produced four puppies when five were ordered. I rang up customer number five, saying I was sorry, and persuaded him with difficulty to take a puppy from a different bitch due in a few week's time. I returned to admire the four puppies the following morning and there were seven! I contacted my customer again, and explained my mistake. I feel sure he suspected me of 'borrowing' some spare puppies!

You shouldn't have to worry about your bitch being short of milk if she is healthy. She may not seem to have very much, but the supply will be stimulated by the puppies' sucking. Even in the event of their being premature, there is generally enough milk for them. Hungry puppies squirm about crying. This sound is entirely different from the contented squeaks and milky gurgles of a happily suckling family, sometimes mistaken by the beginner for hunger.

An old bitch, or one which has been ill during pregnancy may have little or no milk. If you expect to need a foster-mother, start looking for one in plenty of time. They aren't easy to find, and if you get an unsuitable one, the cure may be worse than the disease.

Your vet will be likely to know of a foster mother, as he may be called on to destroy unwanted puppies, but do make sure that the bitch has

'Crunch! Crunch!' Nook as a puppy is certainly not afraid of sheep.

been vaccinated. Spaniels, Labradors and sheepdogs often make good foster mothers. Dogs of terrier type are more likely to take exception to the puppies. The foster mother should be allowed to keep one of her own puppies, and be very careful when you introduce the strangers.

Of course, if your bitch produces a very big litter, and ten is possible, you may decide to put some of them on a foster mother. I have known bitches to rear ten puppies, but as few have ten teats, eight or nine being more usual, it's a hungry job for number ten.

Some people will talk airily about rearing weak young puppies with a milk substitute given through an eye-dropper. Think hard before you embark on this. It is a two-hourly business and success is by no means certain. It is possible to rear puppies by hand from a fortnight old, any younger is dicey.

I dislike writing about having young puppies destroyed, but we all know there are times when it has to be done. One time when the question should not arise is in cases of mix-mating. The bitch shouldn't be allowed to get as far as producing a litter of mongrels. She should be injected after the mix-mating. Destruction is a matter for the vet, especially if the puppies are more than a few hours old. If you breed many dogs, you will get the occasional puppy which is malformed at birth. They are usually stillborn, but not always. A small weak puppy may survive if it has a good mother, but a pup with a crooked leg or any other deformity should be destroyed as soon as possible.

The puppies' eyes will open at ten to fourteen days of age. Again, I have noticed that puppies from a young bitch seem to open their eyes sooner than the others. Once this happens they will creep about a little, but not much, up to three weeks old.

I don't advocate using an infra-red lamp unless the weather is very cold. Generally speaking, bitches don't care for them, and will move the puppies away. One hung in a small building will take the chill off the air even if the puppies aren't directly under it. In really cold weather, it is essential to use one, and the puppies will make for it and lie under it as soon as the mother goes to her food. They will enjoy the warmth, sleep more and grow faster, but beware that they will also be softer and must be hardened off gradually, turning the lamp off for longer and longer periods in the daytime.

The Working Mother

It is surprising how much work some people who are normally humane expect their bitches to do immediately before and soon after whelping. In the sphere of sheepdog trials where one would expect owners to value their dogs, I have seen a bitch running which had been taken away from fortnight old pups, while another whelped in her owner's car on the way home. One would not be allowed to beat or abuse a dog on the trial field and neither should this sort of abuse be allowed.

Some bitches, usually those which go off work when in whelp, continue the strike until the puppies are three or four weeks old, but most seem to enjoy a change of occupation.

Obviously it is still very important that she shouldn't get kicked or knocked about, and neither should she get over tired: if she has a regular routine, for example bringing in cows night and morning, she will be able to return to it within a few days of whelping. Getting overheated is bad for her milk, and she must not be kept away from her family for long at a time. Work is the exercise she is used to, and the easiest way to keep her exercised as long as it isn't overdone.

One important point to remember is not to let her get wet and muddy and return to young puppies without being rubbed dry. If she can't work without getting muddy, don't work her at all. The puppies could easily get chilled and die, or they could develop jaundice.

Many Border Collies put work before everything. Their working instinct has been developed to an extent where it is the mainspring of their existence. Bitches of this dedicated type sometimes make poor mothers. At the sound of sheep on the move, they will jump up, scattering puppies and trampling them underfoot in their anxiety to get back to work.

I have owned some mothers like that, the worst case being a very good bitch called Moyne. Moyne, a handsome smooth-coated bitch with a snowy white stripe across her hips, regularly bred litters of strong healthy puppies and they certainly needed their health and strength. She treated them shamefully, only feeding them when she had nothing better to do. All survived and most were excellent.

Moyne used to live in an open shed near the barn where the ewes were brought in to lamb. She had her first litter of five in a loose box with a door more than five feet high in the front yard. I kept the top door closed until the puppies were a week old, and they were big for their age. A short time afterwards, I saw Moyne jumping out over the door, a puppy in her mouth. Swinging it carelessly, she galloped out of the yard. She had already taken two of them to her old sleeping quarters. I met her coming back for number four. We barricaded her into the chosen building which had no door, and she reared her family in slapdash fashion, always preferring to be at work. I have owned a number of Moyne's descendants, and all were shocking mothers.

The Puppies

Border Collie puppies are remarkably tough little creatures. As I've explained, they often need to be. For three weeks they need no attention, all things going normally. If they are hungry, they will whimper. Silence is a sign that all is well.

At three weeks old, the puppies are wormed for roundworms. These are present in all puppies at birth and can be in lethal quantities. Many a puppy has died, infested with roundworms, from three to six weeks old. I repeat the dose with the quantity doubled at five weeks and again at seven to eight weeks. When dosing young puppies, be gentle. Poke the tablet past the point of no return with your little finger, and wait until you are sure it has gone down. You may feel the puppy swallow, and its tongue will appear. Follow the dose with a little warm milk.

Border Collies don't go in for big litters, but there are exceptions...

If you prefer a liquid wormer, use the barrel of a two cc plastic hypodermic syringe, and give the dose slowly.

No other dosing is necessary provided the puppies are healthy. The most common complaints among young puppies are digestive, and dealt with in the veterinary section. Diarrhoea is common and not necessarily serious. More often than not it is merely a sign of overeating. It should be watched though, since if it continues it may lead to infection and gastroenteritis could follow.

WEANING

Weaning is another subject which is easy to generalise about. Some authorities say with great firmness that it should start at three weeks old. My own opinion is that it should start when the mother's milk supply is no longer adequate. This depends on the bitch and number of puppies. A poor milker with a big litter (six or more) will need assistance before the puppies are three weeks old if they are to get a good start. On the other hand, a bitch with plenty of milk and, say, three puppies, will rear them perfectly well for four to five weeks.

Signs of hunger in the puppies are whimpering and trying to follow the mother when she is fed. The most reliable guide is to pick up each puppy and weigh him in your hand. He should be nicely plump. If you can see his ribs and he opens his mouth seeking food, it's high time he was fed. You can start giving a little milk to the thinner puppies and leave the others a few days longer.

I start the puppies on cows' milk warmed to blood heat. If they are hungry they will drink from a shallow dish held under their chins almost at once. They will also take a little shredded lean beef, although I don't usually give any meat to puppies under four weeks old. The puppy has drunk enough milk when he is full. This sounds like a glimpse of the obvious, but feeding a hungry puppy with milk is rather like filling a hot water bottle. You can feel the little creature swelling up. When he has had enough he will stop drinking, relieve himself and fall asleep.

The puppies can be fed together from a dish as soon as their legs will support them. Their biggest problem at less than four weeks old is falling into the dish, and the hardier spirits wade into the middle, so you must supervise them.

Somewhere around four weeks old, they seem to get the idea all at once, and you need only keep an eye on them to see that one isn't getting pushed out. While the puppies are being fed, take the bitch away and feed her somewhere else. Tie her up if she won't keep away.

On a dairy farm, keep giving cows' milk warmed to blood heat to the puppies, increasing the quantity by degrees, and adding some crumbled brown bread. If you don't keep cows, give a milk substitute.

Don't use a substitute intended for calves as it won't be strong enough. Use one designed for lambs, or else one especially made up for puppies.

Some bitches start to go dry when the puppies are between three and four weeks old, while others keep milking away for five, six or seven weeks. Suddenly taking the puppies away from a mother with a plentiful supply of milk may lead to her getting mastitis as well as being wasteful. The best way is to take her away from the puppies for longer and longer intervals, and get her back to work. The puppies will take more solid food in her absence, and soon weaning will be complete.

PREPARING PUPPIES FOR NEW HOMES

If the puppies are to be sold, they must be completely weaned before they go to their new homes. Your first aim should be to get them all ready together with no weaklings. This means paying special attention to any small puppies. Another important point is that they should be friendly. If there are older children in the family they will see to that, but toddlers should never be allowed to handle young puppies. They are tough, but not so tough that they can stand being dropped on their heads.

In my case, where usually I am the only person handling the puppies, I take every opportunity to pick them up, stroke them and talk to them.

True, they are going to be working dogs, but that is no reason for depriving them of affection. Don't go to the other extreme. Cuddling and baby talk probably do no harm, but make it harder for the puppy to adjust to a new home where his advances may be rebuffed.

Finding homes for the puppies depends a lot on your situation. Most Border Collies are happiest doing farm work and perhaps competing in sheepdog trials which are an extension of farm work. Some may be trained for obedience and other forms of competition, or for activities such as rescue work. Some make delightful pets and companions, but they are a minority. I do not say categorically that Border Collies don't make good pets. But then, they don't all make good workers either. There are misfits in both camps. Some dogs bred, reared and sold for work are useless. They have missed their vocation, and would be much happier lying by the sitting-room fire. It is sadder still to see a dog whose whole brain and being are centred on the work he was bred for, perhaps living in a city flat and being taken out for a short walk on a lead. Such dogs suffer agonies of frustration, and may become neurotic. One such acquired the habit of running 'round and 'round in circles, biting his own tail and occasionally jumping in the air. He returned to his farmer breeder, but the damage was done and he was incurable. He started to work sheep well, but would return to his interminable circling and jumping as soon as he was out of the field. Finally, he had to be destroyed.

Much depends on the strain you are breeding. A knowledge of the natures of sire and dam is your only guide. If they are both good workers, you should look for farm homes and advertise in the farming papers. Advertising isn't cheap, which is another reason for getting your puppies ready to go within a short space of time. It's a false economy to save money by putting your advertisement in a paper with a small circulation. The national farming papers will be read by most farmers in search of a puppy likely to make a working dog.

Advertisements should be simple and honest. Avoid superlatives—they won't be believed anyway. Words like 'adorable' when applied to puppies cause most farmers to pass on hastily to the next advertisement. The type I have found successful would read something like this:

For sale to good farm homes, 6 pedigree Border Collie pups. Healthy and well reared. Parents excellent with cattle and sheep. Mother may be seen working. Tel. no.

Don't go into the breeding unless it is so well known that it is likely to be familiar to the average layman: 'Sire won International,' 'Dam won on TV'. Never say the puppies are certain to be good workers or natural workers. Buyers could come back and complain if they are disappointed, and it wouldn't necessarily be the dog's fault if he was unsatisfactory.

Some breeders accept a deposit. This isn't such a good idea as it sounds. The customer may be slow to collect his puppy, thinking that you might as well feed it for him for a few more weeks. If he has paid part of the price, you can't sell it elsewhere. Always collect your money before you part with your dog, assuming you are dealing with strangers.

Sending a puppy by rail should be avoided if possible, but sometimes there is no alternative. If you do, put him in a fairly small box, as puppies travel better if they have limited space. Put a newspaper folded flat in the bottom, with a little clean straw on top. Put your own name and telephone number on the box as well as those of the recipient, and the name of the railway station it is going to. Make sure that the station staff label the box 'livestock' and don't leave it in the station. Wait for the train and see it actually put in the guard's van.

Don't send puppies by rail in sultry or very cold weather. Feed the puppy well the night before he travels, but give him only a small drink of milk an hour before he travels. Check his coat for fleas a day or two before he goes. Write a letter to the new owner explaining what food the puppy is getting, what doses he has received and the date when his inoculations are due. Tape this to the travelling box.

I don't think it's fair to charge the same money for a puppy at six weeks as at ten weeks. If they aren't all gone at eight weeks or a little more, try to keep the others on until they show some 'eye' and grow out of the puppy stage at about four months old, and advertise again, asking more.

By this time, they will have cost a great deal more, and will have got their inocculations. From eight to twelve weeks old is an expensive time in a puppy's life.

THE PUPPIES YOU DECIDE TO KEEP

I beleive that it's a good idea to keep two and dispose of one later on. At six weeks or so, get your puppies out of doors, weather permitting. Up to six weeks old they will get what exercise they need playing in their sleeping quarters. After that, you should lose no time in teaching them their names and getting them familiar with their surroundings.

NAMING THE PUPPY

The International Sheep Dog Society will accept only short working type names nowadays. This is to discourage the flights of fancy of breeders whose Border Collies are intended for the show ring. The old Stud Books are full of strange names: Bobo, Towzer…I won't upset you by going on. It's nice to come across a name that is short and 'callable' yet different. Unless there is a prefix, the Bens, Roys and Nells are a researcher's nightmare, although I quite realise this is not the farmer's problem. The habit persists of naming the puppy after its sire or dam as appropriate. Thank goodness the I.S.D.S. put a stop to the practice of allowing two or more puppies in a litter to be given the same name.

There is a convention in the naming of working dogs. Certain names keep their popularity year in, year out. Ben, Lad, Roy and Cap are classic names for dogs, while the favourites for bitches include Nell, Meg, and Jess.

Even since the insistence on short names, there have been oddities. I myself have been asked to register Zam, Zen, Zaphod, Ash, Quarry and Yorkie. I drew the line at Zonk.

Some people favour a place. Crohane and Corrib are examples. Not everyone's choice but better than flower names—Bluebell, Snowdrop, Daisy and the popular Rose sound more like cows to me.

As for joke names like Help, I feel the joke must wear out long before the dog. If you breed many puppies, it's a good idea to keep a notebook containing suitable names to guide dithering buyers, and also to list names you have used yourself, so you can use a numeral for repeats.

CARE OF THE BITCH AFTER WEANING

Male dogs cast their coats once a year in the spring, bitches cast theirs after rearing puppies. The process always has an adverse effect on a dog and can make him off colour, and likewise the bitch which has already produced and reared a litter. The bitch usually comes in season at the time her new coat starts to grow, so she is in her full coat when the puppies are born. Some smooth bitches develop bare patches on their thighs around weaning time, and often a heavy-coated bitch will lose hair until she is almost unrecognisable.

This puts an added strain on the system, and if in addition she is working stock, she will need generous feeding and a good tonic. The extra feeding should be continued until the puppies are three to four months old. Around then the coat starts to grow, and the bitch may come in heat again. No wonder breeding at every season soon leads to small litters!

A well-known sheepdog handler, owner of a trial-winning bitch, was worried because she was running badly. He mentioned it to his wife, whose lack of interest in dogs was total. Her comment was, 'You don't expect a hen in moult to lay eggs, do you?' The bitch's owner saw the truth of the remark and rested her for a while. Her new coat grew and she recovered her form.

The bitch should be wormed as soon as the puppies are weaned, as she will have been reinfected by her puppies. The dose should be repeated after six weeks or so.

Penny pinching in the matter of food is always bad policy with working dogs. If you are breeding from the dogs you work, it is madness.

If you give plenty of nourishing food, treat your bitch kindly and sensibly and are meticulous in dosing and inoculating both her and her puppies, you will soon be rewarded not only by a ready sale for puppies but also by the dogs' looks and performance.

Prevention and Treatment of Illness

This chapter doesn't pretend to be a comprehensive veterinary guide. Diagnosis and treatment of serious complaints should be left to a qualified vet, and you should never buy antibiotics or vaccines from an unqualified person.

A properly looked-after Border Collie is usually free of health problems, at least until he grows old: provided he has been inoculated, it should seldom be necessary to call the vet. You should know when he ought to be called, and when you can deal with the trouble yourself. There are cases when time lost seeking veterinary advice could lead to an unnecessary death, so all owners should have an elementary knowledge of first aid and emergency treatment. Don't forget, however, that veterinary treatment changes all the time, so consult your vet when in doubt. Advances in medicine are made every year, and drugs and antibiotics change too.

By the nature of his work, a Border Collie is exposed to minor injuries, dirt, wet and the proximity of sick farm animals. He may also pick up parasites from sheep and cattle. It is up to you to care for him by keeping him clean and dry when not working, by regular 'boosters' against disease, and by the simple rules laid out earlier. In particular, see that your dog is not physically overtaxed in his work. If he has to work hard, he must be fed accordingly. It is much easier to slim a Border Collie than to build him up—the breed uses so much nervous energy. We all know that a dog in poor condition is a target for chills and infections that wouldn't affect a fit animal.

THE KILLER DISEASES

Distemper and Hardpad; Virus Hepatitis; Leptospirosis; Parvovirus

No cared-for dog should fall victim to any of these. Your vet will advise you about vaccination. The usual method is to inoculate against all these diseases at twelve weeks, and follow up with a second shot for leptospirosis at fourteen weeks. Boosters should be given annually. All these diseases are killers and leptospirosis also affects cattle and human

Proper veterinary care will ensure a happy and healthy start for your pup.

beings. The distemper vaccine is not given at less than twelve weeks unless there is an epidemic, and then only under veterinary supervision. The others can be protected against much younger, but the dose must be repeated at twelve weeks to give full immunity.

Parvovirus, only around since 1976, has been the biggest problem in recent years, but anxiety about parvo should not blind you to the dangers of distemper, which breaks out regularly in areas where there are neglected dogs straying, or leptospirosis, which is spread by the urine of rats and can easily be picked up in farm buildings. Never leave uneaten food about, as it encourages rats.

Vaccination is troublesome and expensive, but not as troublesome and expensive as an outbreak of disease. Even when not fatal, they are all difficult to cure, painful and distressing for the dog, and can put a kennel permanently out of business. Prevention is better than cure, in fact failure to prevent is more than careless, it is madness. You should not vaccinate a sick dog, and, in fairness to others, you should bring the vet to the dog rather than take an infected animal to his clinic.

Distemper is a horrible, protracted disease, often fatal. Any veterinary book will describe the symptoms, and any owner having had to deal with a dog suffering from distemper will take care it doesn't happen again. Almost as bad as the disease itself are the side effects. Brain damage is common and causes chorea, fits, convulsions, blindness and disorientation. Fortunately distemper can be prevented from spreading by conventional disinfectants and routine hygiene.

Parvovirus is curable except in young puppies, depending on the form the disease takes. The type that affects the heart is always fatal as the animal merely drops dead. The more usual form is often mistaken for gastroenteritis, involving a bloody scour and frothy vomit. Any gastric complaint with this type of symptom is a case for the vet who will prescribe antibiotics. There is a fair chance of recovery. A dog can get parvovirus only once, but it should be remembered that he can transmit the disease for up to six weeks after the scour clears up.

Parvo is resistant to normal antiseptics. A strong bleach or toilet disinfectant containing chloros is the best thing for disinfecting buildings. Parvo is extremely hard to get rid of once it has occurred in a kennel. If you have lost a dog with the disease and want to replace him, get the new dog inoculated, and ask the owner to keep him another fortnight. It is worth paying him to do this. The next best thing is isolation for a fortnight in a rigorously disinfected building away from your other dogs, but the disease is so easily carried and transmitted that this is not always satisfactory.

Some dogs get parvo lightly and appear to have made a complete recovery, but beware of side effects. Distemper affects the brain, parvo the heart. The dog's constitution may be undermined so that he is no use for work and may die suddenly. He may be thin and listless and not respond to tonics. Other dogs recover completely, and all victims are immune for the rest of their lives.

Never neglect inoculation, even if you live on a mountain ten miles from the nearest village. Nobody knows how virus diseases lie dormant and then appear suddenly, apparently from nowhere, but they do.

SOME COMMON AILMENTS

Accidents

A dog which has been run over by a car or injured by stock may be too hurt and terrified to handle. You should muzzle him before trying to move him or expecting your vet to examine him. An effective and simple way is to tie a piece of tape around his muzzle with the knot under his jaw and fasten it behind his ears. Fetch the vet to the dog if possible, rather than the other way round. If the dog must be moved, lift him on a piece of hardboard or other rigid object. Even a sack or coat is better to lift him on than carrying him in your arms.

If you suspect broken bones or internal bleeding, move the dog as little as possible, and cover him up warmly to counteract shock. Don't attempt to give him brandy or medicine.

Anaemia

Iron deficiency, mainly found in breeding bitches. The dog is listless and its gums are pale. You can get a suitable iron tonic from any chemist, and a little raw liver can be added to the diet.

Bleeding

Put a thick cotton wool dressing over the wound, or if not available, a large handkerchief folded into a pad, bandage into place tightly, and get the dog to the vet as quickly as possible.

Cancer

Occasionally met with even in young dogs. It is usually best to have the dog put down.

Chorea

A side effect of distemper, similar to St. Vitus's dance in humans. Sometimes the dog has fits and convulsions. In milder cases, twitching or jerking the limbs is the only symptom. There is no cure.

Collie Eye Anomoly

see Hereditary conditions.

Distemper

see Killer diseases.

Eczema

May be hereditary, in which case it often appears in spring and autumn. No cure, but may be relieved by using a preparation. When not a hereditary condition, eczema may be caused by too many carbohydrates in the diet or by over-rich food. A change of diet should cure this, and a dessertspoonful of cooking oil in the food will provide essential fat and work wonders for a dull scurfy coat. Often a bitch will lose hair and her skin will be scurfy when she is rearing a litter. This is due to a hormonal imbalance and will right itself without treatment.

Gastroenteritis

Commonest in puppies, and often mistaken for parvovirus. It usually starts as an ordinary digestive complaint due to over-eating, then infection sets in. Vomiting and scouring are danger signals and should never be ignored. The vet may prescribe antibiotics. Not all antibiotics can be safely kept, especially in liquid form. *Never* keep tablets in envelopes or paper bags, and *always* check expiration dates. Some medicines and vaccines should be kept in the fridge.

Hardpad

Associated with distemper. *See* Killer diseases.

Heat Stroke

A dog left in the sun in a car may succumb to heat stroke quickly. The glass conducts the heat—you wouldn't stay in the car yourself with the windows shut. A working Border Collie can also get heat stroke if he has to work hard in hot weather. A willing dog may work until he collapses. He should be immersed in cold water if there's a tank or bath handy. If not, pour cold water over him and give him a drink. This nearly always results in a quick recovery.

Heart Attack

A dog which has had a heart attack shouldn't be expected to work stock again. Treatment may keep the dog in good health for years, so you need not have your dog destroyed. He can lead a happy and useful life as companion and guard, but violent exertion is out.

Hip Dysplasia

see Hereditary conditions.

Hysteria

Fits, said to be connected with an ingredient formerly used in white bread. Hysteria can also be a side effect of distemper, or a hereditary complaint. An affected dog should be given sedatives.

Kennel Cough

A contagious disease which spreads like wildfire where dogs are kept in crowded conditions. I haven't known it to affect working dogs, but it could of course be picked up at a show or in a strange kennel. Treat with antibiotics.

Kennel Lameness

A result of too much carbohydrate in the diet. Common among dogs fed on porridge, biscuit or flake maize. Easily cured by adding meat and vegetable matter to the diet.

Leptospirosis

see Killer diseases.

Mange

Most types can be cured by clipping the dog and washing him with silica gel. These washes are poisonous, and you must take all the precautions advised by the makers.

Demodectic mange, sometimes called follicular mange, is harder to deal with. It is said to be carried by certain bitches who pass it on to some of their male puppies, and is caused by a burrowing mite. Until recently, demodectic mange could only be eased, not cured. A drug has been perfected which cures the majority of cases. This disease is not contagious, but some types of mange can be passed on to humans in the form of scabies.

Mastitis

An infection of the udder. The cause may be too much milk for a small litter, removing the puppies too soon, or scratches made by the puppies' claws or by brambles when working. Either way the infection is a serious matter and must be treated with antibiotics at once. The puppies must be taken off and reared by hand. A bitch which has had mastitis once will probably get it again, and I would consider selling her to someone who didn't require her for breeding.

Untreated, mastitis may lead to mammary tumours or even cancer. Benign lumps in the udder usually disappear. If they don't, a male hormone injection is often effective, otherwise there is no alternative to surgery.

Occasionally, mastitis occurs in early pregnancy. Your vet will be careful in his choice of an antibiotic which will not harm the unborn puppies.

Milk Fever

This is caused by a calcium deficiency in lactating bitches. Staggering is the first symptom, and convulsions may follow. It should not happen to a properly fed bitch and I have never come across a case. It does happen however, and a calcium injection will bring about a miraculous recovery.

Monorchid

This is a dog with only one testicle. The other is still in the abdomen. This is a serious defect, which can lead to cancer and is said to be a result of careless inbreeding. Such a dog may be returned to the seller if bought as an adult with a clean bill of health.

Nephritis

A fairly common kidney complaint of older dogs but far rarer than it used to be. Affected dogs grow thin and apathetic, while smelling strongly of stale urine. There is no permanent cure, but the dog should be encouraged to drink as much water as possible and given plenty of exercise.

Parvovirus

see Killer diseases.

Poisoning

If you think your dog has picked up strychnine, you can give him washing soda, the traditional antidote, in the unlikely case of having any handy. With the exception of Warfarin, most poisons are quick and often agonising killers. Try to make the dog vomit by giving salt and water, a teaspoon of salt to a cupful of water, using fenbendazole preparation. Get the vet immediately, or take the dog to him, whichever is quicker.

Warfarin is an anti-coagulant rat poison. It works by preventing the blood from clotting, so that tiny injuries caused by sharp bits of food or scratches bleed unchecked. Warfarin will kill a dog if he has free access to it, but more often he gets only enough to make him ill. This can be treated successfully if caught in time, but the dog is sure to be anaemic through loss of blood (*see* Anaemia).

Progressive Retinal Atrophy

see Hereditary conditions.

Rickets

A result of calcium deficiency causing deformed leg bones in puppies. It shouldn't happen. Give high-protein diet and cod liver oil. Curable if caught soon enough.

Scour (Diarrhoea)

Sometimes a straightforward digestive upset, sometimes due to a virus. If scour persists or is bloody, consult your vet.

Temperature

A symptom, not a disease, but a dog may run a high temperature for a variety of reasons. Normal for a dog is 101.4° Fahrenheit.

Travel Sickness

Confine the dog in a small area, and prevent him from looking out of the window. Don't feed him within two hours of travelling. Dogs may be given travel sickness pills; your vet will advise on this.

Virus Hepatitis

see Killer diseases.

Vomiting

Like scour, vomiting may be a symptom of something more serious. Dogs vomit easily, and often there seems to be no reason for it. It is just Nature's way of disposing of an unwise meal. If it persists, get the vet, especially if there is blood or froth.

Wasp or Bee Stings

These can be eased by bathing with a cup of warm water in which a tablespoonful of bicarbonate of soda has been dissolved. A bee sting is left behind, and you should remove it if you can find it. The wasp keeps its sting for future use.

Wounds

If not serious enough to need stitching, swab with warm water and dettol (a chloroxylenol solution) or hydrogen peroxide. Normally, the dog will hasten healing by licking the wound, but if it has been stitched or he is trying to bite it, he must be prevented, if necessary, by muzzling.

After reading this section, you may look thankfully at your working Border Collie, thinking him very lucky indeed to be alive. In fact, I have kept Border Collies for many years, and have had few health problems with them. They are not gluttonous feeders, they are seldom fighters, and they have been bred for physical soundness. They don't spare themselves, so an old dog may suffer from rheumatism, heart trouble or both, and they are accident prone as I explained earlier. But as a breed, I think they are as free as most from disease.

If your dog does become ill and is being treated, you can help him to recover by keeping him warm and contented. Treat him like a human invalid, giving him sleeping quarters where he won't be disturbed by loud noises, so that he gets the maximum rest. Keep him supplied with fresh water and keep meals small and appetising. Discourage other people (except the vet) from hanging over the sick dog and petting him, even with the best intentions. Rest, warmth, peace and the reassurance of his master's concern are as necessary to recovery as medicine.

A dog convalescing from an illness needs extra nourishing food. Whatever you do, don't ask your dog to work again until he has fully recovered.

A working Border Collie can get hurt on the job. Being observant can help prevent serious illness.

HEREDITARY CONDITIONS AND DEFECTS

It is incorrect to imagine that working dogs are free from recessive hereditary conditions and congenital defects. Border Collies are freer than many other breeds, because breeders have not aimed at exaggerations in appearance as they have in some types found mainly in the show ring.

Hereditary defects in the Border Collie may be roughly divided into two categories; those which affect working ability and those which do not.

In the first category come deafness, blindness, hip dysplasia, slipping patellas and serious physical deformities. In the second group, we find wall-eyes, extra dew-claws, crooked tails, over and undershot jaws, and undesirable colours.

Somewhere between the two categories comes the defect of sterility. This is a recessive condition unless a result of disease but by its very nature cannot be passed on. Sterile Border Collies, both male and female, are more common than is generally supposed, and there is no apparent reason for the condition.

Sterility is only serious when the dog concerned is a good one, so hundreds of cases are probably never discovered. The owner of an average dog or bitch, if it fails to reproduce more than once, is likely to give up trying and keep quiet. Only when it is a trial winner or exceptionally well bred does the owner persist in trying, usually in vain, sometimes for years, to find a veterinary remedy.

It seems likely that this defect is a result of close breeding in the past. I am certain that persistent linebreeding leads to small litters, and in some cases eventually no litters at all. A clear case of nature putting a stop to things when the breed is about to run into trouble.

Close inbreeding leads to obvious defects. Pure white puppies are suspect as they may be deaf, blind or both. Close breeding is also blamed for congenital cataracts and slipping stifles, two conditions which, although not unknown in Border Collies, are rare enough not to merit consideration here. Both conditions are incurable. Inbred puppies may also be physically deformed at birth, or develop a crippling infirmity in the first few months of life. Their brothers and sisters should not be bred from, no matter how well they work, although they may appear to be perfectly sound themselves. They may carry the defect on, and it will crop up again.

Hip dysplasia is said to be on the increase in Border Collies, but I have no personal experience of an affected dog. As long as our Collies continue to do the work they were originally designed for, such defects will be obvious from an early age, and the affected dogs will not be allowed to breed. Trouble creeps in when the dogs lead such sedentary lives that their limitations don't show up, and they are allowed to propagate.

PRA and CEA

By far the most serious hereditary condition in working Border Collies is P.R.A. (progressive retinal atrophy) sometimes called night blindness. In Border Collies, this defect is said to come from inter-breeding with setters long ago. PRA has been familiar to breeders of setters for many years, but some top-class trial Collies had become affected before breeders

Knowing your Border Collie's lineage can keep him from passing on hereditary diseases.

became aware of the danger. The International Sheep Dog Society started testing dogs which competed in National Trials back in the sixties, while other breeders were encouraged to have their dogs tested at subsidised rates. The results were alarming, up to 14 percent of tested dogs failing to pass.

The disease, as its name denotes, is progressive. It cannot be diagnosed with certainty at less than two years old, and slightly affected dogs worsen with age. Some never become totally blind, other go blind at three or four years old.

It was assumed that only one type of PRA was involved, the type passed direct from parent to progeny. Such a disease could be stamped out, and the Society's system of testing and reduced registration fees for progeny tested puppies had lowered the incidence to 1 percent.

Recently, it became evident that a recessive form of the disease was also to be found among Borders, and measures have now been tightened up to include the retesting of dogs which compete in National Trials each year. While the I.S.D.S. accepts a clear test at two years, the Kennel Club require three years.

PRA is found in a large number of breeds, and the Kennel Club won't give the 'all clear' until five years in the case of Cocker Spaniels, English Springers, Smooth Dachshunds and Miniature and Toy Poodles.

When the incidence of PRA was at its height among Border Collies, every case of blindness was attributed to it by nervous breeders. In fact some dogs will always go blind in old age from cataracts, glaucoma or other eye diseases, and blindness can also be a side effect of distemper.

There is no treatment for these cases, nor is there any for PRA

An affected dog may go blind very slowly and manage to work as long as he is in familiar surroundings. A trained dog may work although totally blind, but it is the height of cruelty to take one into unfamiliar surroundings, or allow him to work stock which may attack him.

PRA was first discovered in Rough Collies in the late 1920s, but it was not until after World War II that the first scientific papers on the subject appeared, and it was another twenty-one years before the British Veterinary Association set up a control scheme with the co-operation of the Kennel Club and the International Sheep Dog Society.

While all concerned were congratulating themselves on the success of the scheme, another form of blindness had appeared among Border Collies. This was CEA, or Collie eye anomaly. It has been a major bogey for some time among Rough Collies, especially in the U.S.A., and, being recessive, will be very hard to eradicate. As said before, recessive conditions can crop up after many generations, so sweeping measures are not always practicable. The I.S.D.S. has extended its scheme to cover CEA, and affected dogs have their registration cancelled.

Fortunately, CEA is comparatively uncommon in Border Collies, and, unlike PRA, it can be diagnosed in puppyhood. It is a constant condition, sometimes causing blindness and sometimes not. One of the dangers of CEA is a predisposition to detached retina, especially in active working dogs which have to gallop and jump.

Probably the seeds of both these forms of blindness were sown generations ago by haphazard and indiscriminate inbreeding. Serious breeders must give thought to the best means of breeding sound stock without jettisoning some of the most illustrious strains in the stud book.

Defective Temperament

Temperament flaws may be due to environment or ill treatment. They may also be due to hereditary defects, and when this is the case, there is nothing to be done. Recessive traits in temperament are extreme nervousness, neurosis and vice. All sorts of things can turn a naturally bad-tempered dog into a vicious one, but when there is no cause for the temper, and it can't be controlled, you may be sure that it is a legacy from some long-dead ancestor.

There is no cure for real viciousness. Punishment makes the dog worse. He will probably be unreliable even with his master. I say 'he', but if 'he' is a 'she' the case is even more hopeless. This is not a common problem among Border Collies, but I have come across it. We bought a young unregistered dog which worked well, but kept attacking the other dogs. We tied him up and hoped he would improve. One day, when loose, he attacked a young bitch, and had mauled her badly before my husband managed to get him away (by twisting his collar and half choking him). I picked up the bitch and had to take refuge in a stable. This dog never attacked humans, but he had a sister which bit several people, including her owner. Both dogs had to be destroyed, and I discovered later that the fault lay in their breeding, their parents being sister and brother. It is to be hoped that no one would breed from such a dog.

There are several common recessive conditions which, while they may be unsightly, don't interfere with a working Border Collie's usefulness. A borderline case is the fairly common overshot jaw. This only affects a dog's work if he needs to bite. It would be most undesirable in a cattle dog. Breeding from a dog or bitch with this defect establishes the fault, even if the puppies have correct mouths. I have dwelt on this fault because it is looked on with indulgence by some breeders in an otherwise good dog. You shouldn't forget that besides being ugly, uneven jaws cannot bite properly. If the front teeth don't meet correctly, the back ones are bound to be out of alignment as well. A tooth with no opposite number to meet it may grow into the opposite gum.

Some Border Collies are born with the tip of the tail curved to one side, while a great old timer, Willie Murphy's Toss, had a tail whose end curled right 'round on itself. There is a strong prejudice against crooked tails, but I know of some top-class dogs with this fault and one very successful trial dog with no tail at all. The trouble here is that if you breed from two animals which carry the fault, the condition may crop up in an aggravated form. The dog's tail may be curled right round like a pig's or stand away sideways from his body at an angle. Nobody would want a dog with such an ugly fault unless he was sold cheaply or given away.

Another common recessive feature is the extra dewclaw or 'spur' on the inside of the hind leg. These can be removed with sharp scissors soon after birth. My old trial dog Billy, although he didn't have them himself, sired one puppy with spurs in almost every litter, so a lot of bitches must carry the fault. I have heard it described variously. 'A sign of mixed breeding,' 'a sign of descent from Scottish dogs whose extra claws helped to prevent them from sinking in soft snow,' 'a sign of bad temper,' and 'a lucky claw'. I have no idea which if any of these is right, but I believe they are less common than they were some years ago.

'Wall-eyes,' or blue eyes are so common among working Border Collies that they are generally accepted without comment, although the breed standard tolerates them only in blue merles. They make no difference to the sight, and many a top-class trial dog has possessed a 'chine' or 'chaney' eye, as many farmers call them. Personally, I don't like the look of them because, like light-coloured eyes, they lack depth of expression. I feel that to refrain from breeding from wall-eyed dogs would be throwing out the baby with the bathwater. I have two myself, neither of which produce wall-eyed puppies, while the brown-eyed Dale sired dozens of them.

There is a risk in breeding from two wall-eyed dogs that some of the puppies may be blind. For that reason breeders of Rough Collies don't as a rule mate two blue merles.

Never forget that a recessive condition can skip as many as ten generations, and it may not be possible to identify it even then. The 'lethal factor' which occasionally causes whole litters to be stillborn can't be passed on in any way the layman can understand, any more than sterility.

It is virtually impossible to 'breed out' a recessive defect. The best you can do is to avoid mating the animals in question a second time. If you do, the fault, whatever it is, is likely to affect more puppies than it did the first time.

The Working Partnership

THE 'PACK LEADER' THEORY

John Holmes's 'pack leader' theory explains much about the psychology of the working Border Collie. In his book *The Farmer's Dog*, he explains how the dog, a pack animal, needs a leader. Without one he is a rudderless vagrant, unless he happens to be a pack-leader type himself. It is up to the dog's master to be his own personal pack leader, to be obeyed and respected at all times.

As for the pack-leading dog, he is not necessarily the best worker. Intelligence is needed for work but the natural leader may be too clever by half, certain of his own rightness, and unwilling to take orders. Holmes points out that most people can work a submissive dog, but a dominant dog requires a dominant personality in his handler.

I had seen all these points demonstrated many times before I read the simple explanation; then everything fell into place in my mind.

I wrote earlier of having a 'way with dogs': the ability to command their respect and affection. Respect without affection achieves passable results workwise, affection in the dog without respect for his handler is worthless when difficulties arise. The dog who loves his master but doesn't respect him will work hard to please that master, but in a crisis the dog, thinking himself superior, will do as he thinks best and disregard orders.

The ability to command respect in a highly intelligent and courageous dog isn't something that humans can necessarily recognise. Without it, the dog will assert his own personality and become boss. Punishment won't alter this. You can't bludgeon a dog into working, and as long as he refuses to work from defiance, he is disobeying and proving himself master. Such a dominant dog will take a beating and continue to disobey the master he has learned to despise rather than fear. Once he is in the field, the dog is on his own. He knows he can't be touched, and the more distance he puts between himself and his handler, the safer he feels. There must be some link other than fear of punishment between the handler and the dog at the far end of the field. An old country proverb says, 'Love will draw you further than gunpowder will throw you'. Respect and affection. Neither is enough by itself. When the partnership is sound, the dog becomes an extension of his master's will, able to anticipate his wishes in an almost uncanny way.

Top handler Julie Simpson, the first woman ever to win the Supreme International Championship. Photo by Ray Kennedy.

WOMEN AS DOG HANDLERS

Throughout this book, I have referred to man and dog—the dog being referred to as "he." Even in this age of equality, we haven't yet had to rename that programme *One Person and Their Dog*. The use of "their," when constantly repeated, grates on the ear, while he/she is horrible, and I hate calling any creature as sensible and sensitive as a Border Collie "it." I asked my agent what he thought, and he said that the British Statute clarifies that "man" embraces *women* too. This sounds as good a reason as another for sticking to the masculine pronouns.

Although women outnumber men in the ranks of show-dog breeders and in many other dog-related activities, they are still in a minority as farmers and sheepdog handlers. Again, television has had a big part in bringing women to the fore: Katy Cropper having won on TV and Viv Billingham having been second. These successes are probably better known to the general public than Julie Deptford's remarkable achievements on the trial field. Many people still think of trialing as a sport strictly for the men.

As far back as 1977, a woman, Jean Hardisty, won the English National Trial. This was reported patronisingly at the time. "They (the judges) fell for the fatal charms of two ladies— Jean Hardisty and Flash," reported the ISDS newsletter. A warm tribute to their performance was followed by a suggestion that the sheep "were just a bit more responsive" by the end of the second day.

Thirteen years later, Julie Deptford was the first woman to get into the final of the Supreme International Championship, having won the qualifier. Attitudes had changed, and although emphasis was naturally put on this new record for women, Julie Deptford's performance was assessed on its merits and not treated like a fluke.

In 1996 the unimaginable happened! Julie Deptford, now Julie Simpson, went one better and won the Supreme International Championship. There has been no suggestion that she was not the deserving winner—praise for her has been generous indeed. The very

Handlers often use a stick or crook to direct the sheepdog.

fact that her success was greeted with no astonishment is also significant. She had already shown that she was capable of winning. When women make up their minds to excel in any sporting field, they are often confined to competing only against other women. Showjumping and sheepdog trialling are two exceptions which spring to mind. And while the horsey scene has as many female competitors as male, the sheepdog scene has not. I foresee a big rise in the number of women competing at sheepdog trials in the coming years. Today those who do take part are very good indeed. Besides those mentioned, there are others who can compete with the best.

In Ireland, women are rarely seen on the trial field. One of the exceptions, Janet Helleris, a consistent winner, had the honour of being the first woman to judge at a National Trial in 1985. An article about Janet was entitled, "Competing in a Man's World." When I interviewed her, she remarked that trialing is one of the few sports where men and women compete on level terms. It compares with sailing in that respect.

Judgment is more important than physical strength. There is no reason why a woman shouldn't go to the very top in trialing and that was proved positively in the 1990s.

Still more would compete, I'm sure, if there was more incentive. The number of woman shepherds is increasing yearly, but woman farmers who work their dogs on the land are still a tiny percentage. Some women who work their dogs as a matter of course at home are self-conscious and afraid of making fools of themselves in a male-dominated sport. This is partly because women seem to find whistling harder to master than men do, while the female voice raised to carry to the far end of the course is apt to emerge not as a shout but as a piercing shriek.

To return to the pack-leader theory, I feel that a woman is at a disadvantage with a dominant type of dog. To offset this, however, a sensitive dog will sometimes work beautifully for a woman and refuse to perform for a man. I've noticed that quite a few women prefer a bitch to a dog, and this may be due to a greater affinity with another female. Bitches are usually more sensitive than dogs, and they are certainly more easily spoiled.

I have never met a woman who could deal with a true pack-leading type of dog: keen dogs, yes; problem dogs, certainly; but not the loner. Yet, to be fair, the majority of men can't manage these dogs either.

DOGS AND THEIR MASTERS

A controversy continues wherever Border Collies are found, as to whether they are better or worse than they used to be. I don't know the answer to that, but most are agreed that good handlers are scarcer than they were.

Probably this is partly due to the hectic pace of life in the twentieth century. Training a dog properly isn't a thing that can be hurried, and beware the trainer who boasts of his quick results. Short cuts in training may produce good results but often they are only temporary. In fact, most good trainers are reticent, and not inclined to boast at all. A moderately good Border Collie with a brilliant handler will win far more prizes on the trial field than a brilliant dog with a moderate handler, and it is rare to hear a really good handler make excuses. When someone leaves the field after a bad run blaming his dog, the judge, the sheep and the weather, take his remarks with a grain of salt. It's more than possible that he himself is at fault. Most good handlers are good losers.

Border Collies, with their extra sensitivity, know exactly how their masters are feeling. You may fool your best friend as you pat your dog saying, 'You can't win them all—it wasn't Roy's fault.' Roy knows perfectly well that you are thinking, 'I wish I'd never seen the useless brute.' He'll forgive you. You can't help your thoughts.

What you mustn't do is to set out on a training session in a bad temper. If something or somebody has upset you, if you feel angry, unhappy or ill, it will pay you to leave the dog at home. The dog knows what you are feeling like, but thinks all your emotions have to do with him. It is too much for a dog to understand that you are angry or frightened or unhappy, but that your feelings have nothing to do with him. Also you may make the fatal mistake of losing your temper.

Punishment

Physical punishment should never be necessary. Do your best to see that the occasion for punishment doesn't arise. A sensitive dog is sufficiently punished by his owner's angry voice. You should avoid striking your dog not only because it seldom does any good but also because you will make him nervous of a stick. I have seen dogs on the trial field who worked well at a distance but wouldn't shed or pen. This tells its own story. The best way to punish a dog is to catch him by the collar and shake him, while telling him off in a low angry voice, unlike the tone you normally use. This is enough for all but the ultra-thick-skinned. Be positive before taking such a step that the dog is disobeying deliberately, and catch him in the act, whatever it is. If you delay the punishment, the dog won't know what it's for.

Reward

Such is the nature of the average Border Collie that a kind word is reward enough for work well done. The dog knows when you are pleased with him, just as surely as he knows when you are angry. If you are in a good mood and everything seems to be going your way, the chances are that your dog will work well, because you are giving him confidence. A few words of praise and a pat are all the reward a trained dog needs. Make a fuss of your dog at home if you like, but don't overdo it at work, or he will be looking for praise instead of getting on with his job.

Dogs being trained for obedience tests need constant praise and games to avoid boredom. The beauty of working stock with a dog is that he is never bored. His work is his play, he needs no other pastime. Border Collies also enjoy jumping and retrieving. It's a good idea to train your working dog to jump on command so that he can get over sheep-proof fences.

Working with your Border Collie should be enjoyable for both of you, and the more enjoyment you get out of the work the better you will both carry it out.

BORDER COLLIES ABROAD

Our working dogs have travelled far from the Scottish borders from which they take their name. They increase in popularity every year in countries all over the world.

Sometimes they have been slow to catch on, because they were exported without sufficient explanation of their ways and needs. The spread of tape recordings, television and video tapes has helped to rectify this.

In countries like Australia and New Zealand, there are other herding dogs besides the Border. The Australian Heeler, the Huntaway, the Kelpie all claim to have their roots in Scotland, and probably have common ancestors with the Borders. Often Border Collies, Kelpies and Huntaways work together among the vast flocks of sheep.

Borders were part of the way of life of the Falkland Islanders with their sheep-based economy. The trial at Port Stanley was a popular annual event. Young dogs have been exported to replace those which were killed in the Falklands War.

In South Africa, Border Collies, introduced by Lionel Pennefather from Ireland in the '30s, are immensely popular, and sheepdog trials draw big crowds. In Canada and the U.S.A., there is a lot of emphasis on working cattle as well as sheep. Trials and exhibitions grow more numerous every year.

Nearer to home, most West European countries have at least some Border Collies. They are exported, among other places, to Holland, France, Switzerland, Germany and Scandinavia. In many countries they are replacing dogs which merely drove stock and did not have the gathering instinct.

In France, the sheepdog trials cater separately for Border Collies and the native Briards, each breed having its staunch adherents. The Briard is a large heavy-coated dog, totally unlike a Border Collie.

Greater understanding of the Border is leading to greater popularity year by year. Long may it last.

THE IDEAL PARTNERSHIP

It is hard to write simply about a complex subject. The owner/trainer needs more than anything else common sense, and after that patience. The common sense should tell you when you have backed a loser. Your dog is a worker but you can't get on. Patience and persistence can work wonders—no working partnership can succeed without some give and take. You can do much to correct your dog's faults, especially if you take the trouble to discover why he misbehaved in the first place. Remember though that his basic nature cannot be altered any more than your own. A bad handler blames his dog, but don't forget that you and your dog may be at odds through an unalterable fault in the dog's make up. You can't, as I said, change your own nature, but you can and should change your dog's. Somebody somewhere will be looking for just such a Collie as the one you can't get on with.

You might try a good trainer if the dog is only disobedient and unruly, but if the trouble is rooted in the dog's inability to understand you, or your own lack of confidence, the benefit will be temporary.

You must not hope your dog will obey you—you must know he will. Walk away—do you look around to see if he is following? You should know he is. Until you can relax, secure in the knowledge that you will be obeyed, you are miles away from a sound working relationship. If you are relaxed and cool, the dog will take his cue from you, and his work will show it. If you are tense and anxious, you will have to deal with a tense, anxious dog. This will lead in turn to a flock of tense, anxious sheep, and the task will be twice as hard as it need be.

Sell your dog to a cool relaxed character, and buy yourself one with a placid nature. Don't wait until the dog has had time to grow fond of you (nothing to do with his attitude to work). The sooner a basic mistake is put right, the better, and you will both be much happier.

Once you find a dog to suit you, you won't be tempted to sell. I can think of no more rewarding partner in the animal kingdom than a good working Border Collie.

Part Two:
The Border Collie
in America

by Carole L. Presburg

About Our Guest Author

Carole Presberg runs a small sheep farm in Massachusetts with the help of her husband Pres and three Border Collies, Moss, Bess, and Flash. She has owned and worked Border Collies for almost 20 years. Publisher and editor of *The Shepherd's Dogge*, a quarterly journal of the Border Collie, and a member of the Dog Writers Association of America, Ms. Presberg has also written numerous articles and short stories for a variety of sheep, wool, and sheepdog publications. She is the founder of the North American Border Collie Rescue Network. In a previous life, she had been a fiber artist and a partner in a small sheep and wool tour of Scotland, but this life does not afford the time for those particular pursuits.

Acknowledgments

I am honored to have been asked to write an American section for *The Working Border Collie* by its author Marjorie Quarton, and I hope it lives up to her expectations.

I could not have completed this project without help from numerous people—my husband Pres, for his continued encouragement and support; Nancy Garden of Carlisle, Massachusetts, for insights into the publishing industry; Nancy Keller of Corydon, Indiana, for her invaluable assistance with the history of the Border Collie in the U.S.A.; Patricia Sides from New York City, for research at the AKC Library; Florence Feldman-Wood of Andover, Massachusetts, for her research through the public library card catalogs; Linda Rorem of Pacifica, California, for a continual supply of data on the early "collies" in this country; Martha McHardy of British Columbia, for her cooperation on Canadian information; and Jane Porter of Greenacres, Washington, a virtual gold mine on the history and culture surrounding the Border Collie, for exceeding my expectations with magnanimous sharing of material. To each, my heartfelt appreciation. Thanks also to numerous people who generously contributed photos of their dogs or provided information or counsel. I cannot thank you each separately, but you know who you are. Apologies to those who sent photos that did not get used. They were greatly appreciated, but unfortunately, we could not use them all. And finally, to my Border Collies— Woolgather Moss, Bess CGC, Flash CGC, and most of all, the ghosts of Highland's Willy Scott and Watermoon Jute, — you were my inspiration. Thank you all.

American Borders

I got my first Border Collie before I had sheep. A spinner and weaver, I decided I had to have my own flock and went to a sheep-and-wool festival to see what breeds were available in my area. I stayed for the sheepdog trials and I was hooked. I had to have one of those incredible dogs!

I am not alone in my infatuation with the Border Collie. The breed is getting so much publicity in the United States today that it is becoming extremely popular. It appears with alarming frequency in television and magazine advertisements. Well-meaning authors, writing for the popular press, are introducing the breed to the general public. Television talk shows feature them. The *New York Times* Best-Seller *The Intelligence of Dogs* rated many breeds of dogs on their intelligence, and the Border Collie ranked number one. As a Border Collie rescue volunteer, the most frequent answer I get to my question, "Why do you want a Border Collie?" is "Because they're smart." Will the Border Collie's intelligence be its undoing? Or will its versatility stand it in good stead for the future?

As you read this, keep in mind that the Border Collie is fundamentally a working dog. It is still essentially bred by people who want a dog to herd livestock. I may have acquired my first Border Collie before I had sheep, but my experience will not allow me to recommend that others do the same. A Border Collie needs a job or he gets bored. He can be destructive if there is nothing to interest him. Tied out on a line all day, he will bark incessantly in frustration. Left alone in a house, he may remove the wallpaper in his boredom.

I spent hours with my first Border Collie driving around looking for sheep farms and trying to talk the farmers into letting me train my dog on their sheep. I spent more hours driving to those farms that would allow me to train my dog. Each time we went to work sheep, I had to spend half an hour settling down my excited dog before we could do any work. Eventually, my husband and I moved to a farm and got sheep of our own. All my other Border Collies grew up on a farm, which made them easier to get along with. My experiences with Border Collie rescue tell me that most people are not prepared to own a dog like this.

The Border Collie is a British breed. The breed in America today is virtually indistinguishable from the British Border Collie due to continual replenishment of breeding and working stock from Britain and Ireland.

Carole Presberg working sheep with Willy.

Many issues that affect the breed and its owners in America today, like buying, breeding, care, management and training are the same as, or closely similar to, what they would be in Britain. Since the main portion of this book has covered these topics, I see no reason to repeat them again in this section. We will concentrate on issues that have uniquely shaped the breed in America, as well as the history and use of the breed in America, which has taken many unusual twists and turns. Today in America, many of the best trial dogs are still either imports from England, Ireland, Scotland, Wales, or bred from imported dogs. To understand the complete picture, it will be necessary to study the history of the breed in this country over a long period of time, indeed, throughout the history of the country.

Introduction *129*

Origins and History
of the Breed
in America

Working collies have been imported to America since the beginning of our nation. They were simply called collies or collie dogs. There is a painting of George Washington, bidding farewell to the Marquis de Lafayette at Mount Vernon in 1784, with his family and two dogs. One dog appears to be a spaniel and the other is a collie that would not be seen as different from any Border Collie today. (*Presidential Pets* by Niall Kelly, Abbeville Press, 1992.) Starting at the end of the Civil War, wealthy Americans began to import sheep. Shepherds, sailing to America with their families and collies, were employed to escort the flocks on board the ships and to work on American estates. When the need arose, these shepherds sent home to Britain for the dogs they knew best.

It is difficult to guess what many of these early immigrants may have gone through, sailing to a foreign land aboard ships crowded with people, livestock, and dogs, but one immigrant, albeit arriving at a later date than the shepherds we are speaking of here, wrote a brief description of his family's arrival in Canada:

When our family sailed from Scotland to Canada in 1929, our black and white Border Collie was kept in the hold. After docking in Halifax, we boarded a train without having seen our luggage or dog. The next morning in Montreal, we had to transfer to another station to continue on to Toronto. Because we still hadn't seen our belongings, we questioned the baggage-car crew. To our dismay we were told that a small dog had run off while being transferred to the second train. Just then a porter appeared and announced: 'There's a pile of luggage over on No. 8 platform that might belong to these people. But a little black and white dog is sitting on it and won't let any of us touch it.' (Eoin P. MacIntyre, reprinted with permission from the August 1994 *Reader's Digest*, © 1994 by Reader's Digest Magazines Limited.)

This story had a happy ending, but earlier emigration would have been fraught with greater perils, and the trip would have taken longer. From the middle of the 18th century to the beginning of the 20th,

The author's red-and-white Border Collie, Watermoon Jute, at their farm in Massachusetts.

America expanded west. Great flocks of sheep and herds of cattle were moved. In the east, there were still large tracts of land being grazed by sheep, cattle, and dairy herds. Often, in both the east and west, herds were driven to higher, greener pastures during summer, and to railroad heads or markets. Livestock was managed, usually by men on horseback, with the help of dogs.

When gold was discovered in California in 1849, prospectors quickly depleted the local food supplies, and meat was needed to supply the gold camps. Sheep ranchers in New Mexico ran many trail drives from Santa Fe to the gold fields until the late 1850s. Accounts of the time say that it took seven mounted cowboys to move 1,000 head of cattle. The same number of sheep could be driven by a single herdsman with one good dog. The dogs used were collies. A well-trained dog on those drives did not bark, except to warn of danger, never left the flock, even to chase rabbits, and might protect the flock from predators if necessary.

Sheep ranching in many of the western states was started by Scots from the Borders, bringing with them their sheep and collies. Later, when young men left Scotland to come to America, they were sent, often with one or more trained collies and a letter of introduction, to a Scots sheep rancher— someone who had left Scotland before them and had "made good." Summer pasturage was as it is today—in the high country on public land. Sheep herders worked in summer for food and a wagon

Karim's Buckaroo, CDX, TD, owned by Karen Clanin, working Barbados sheep.

to live in and were paid in the fall with a choice of land, sheep, or cash in any combination. Scots that came in the 1890s with only collies thus had the chance to acquire land and sheep. One of these was Idaho rancher Andy Little, who had been a shepherd in Moffat in the Borders of Scotland. When he was 24 years old, he came to the United States (in 1894) with two dogs, Katie and Jim, and a letter to an Idaho rancher.

Ultimately, Little was to maintain 300,000 sheep and over 1,000 fully trained working collies. He returned to Scotland to buy collies and later, his sons made the same visits home. Some of his imports were blue in color and so well liked that other sheep ranchers and herders in the area soon had blue dogs. Little and other Scots ranchers also had a reputation for their ability to train herding dogs. (*Andy Little, Idaho Sheep King* by Louise Shadduck, Caxton Printers Ltd., Caldwell, Idaho, 1990.)

Eventually, summer shepherding became the work of the Basques, who came to America and worked as contract shepherds, sometimes returning home when they had saved enough money. Often they had no dogs of their own, but instead used the ranchers' dogs. Finally, many Basques also earned land and sheep and began making their mark on America. Dominique Laxalt, the father of a Nevada Governor and United States Senator, was one of them, coming to Nevada at the age of 16 and beginning his herding career with 3,000 sheep and a dog.

Border Collies, descended from these early Western imports, live and work on American ranches today. Many are not registered because their ancestors came here before there was a registry in Britain, but may be as well bred and skilled as the latest imported trial-bred collies.

Above: This Border Collie, Greg and Wendi Carleton's Scotti, worked sheep on a ranch in Merril, Oregon. *Below:* A Border Collie's work is never done. Carleton's Scotti works sheep back at the ranch.

Four American Cousins of the Border Collie

THE OLD-FASHIONED FARM COLLIE

In Britain and Ireland, Border Collies are still just called "collies" by many people. The old working collies of Britain and Ireland were of a variety of types depending on where they came from, what they were used for, or who owned them and what the owner liked. So what is a farm collie? Of the farm collie, Linda Rorem of Pacifica, California, a herding dog historian who breeds standard Collies and Shetland Sheepdogs, and trains herding dogs of all breeds, writes:

"I've been interested in finding an old-fashioned working collie but they seem to have disappeared in the '50s and '60s. I've seen numbers of them in old family albums, books, etc., and have talked to people who remember them. They were similar in type to the show collie at the turn of the century, that is, somewhat in between the Border Collie type and the present very exaggerated show collie. They were used as all-around farm dogs, generally loose-eyed and upright in working style."

Farm collies developed from collies brought to America by farmers from different parts of Great Britain and Ireland, and many older Americans who grew up on farms remember the type. They could never have been called a breed, were never registered, and likely most were not even purebred. Rorem describes "Shep" as being mostly black-and-tan, or sable-and-white, and very similar to the English Shepherd.

THE ENGLISH SHEPHERD

Not to be confused with the Old English Sheepdog (or OES), the English Shepherd, despite its name, is an American breed. Rorem says:

"Its ancestors came to America with settlers from the British Isles. In earlier times it was called simply, 'shepherd dog' and has also been called 'farm collie', 'farm shepherd', and 'American shepherd', but it was the English name that came to be given to the breed."

The breed developed, primarily in the Eastern and Midwestern states, at the turn of the century, from working collie stock. It is generally more stocky and square than the Border Collie, and typically works on its feet

The English Shepherd is generally more stocky and square than the Border Collie of today.

rather than crouching and showing eye like a Border Collie. It is also more generally a heeler and a driving dog. Although many English Shepherds are black-and-white like the Border Collie, black-and-tan or sable-and-white are just as common, as in the farm collie. In fact, many enthusiasts maintain that the English Shepherd *is* the old farm collie or "Shep". Today, the English Shepherd has its own breed club, the English Shepherd Club, and it is registered by the National Stock Dog Registry in Butler, Indiana.

THE AUSTRALIAN SHEPHERD

The Australian Shepherd is perhaps the herding breed most shrouded in mystery. It may have been altogether unknown in Australia, although, according to Kelley, "what are sometimes called German Collies [or Coolies] in [Australia] in America are called Australian sheep dogs." (*Sheep Dogs* by R. B. Kelley, Angus & Roberson, Sydney, 1942). Some enthusiasts maintain that it was brought by Basque shepherds who accompanied flocks of sheep being imported to America from Australia. Likely, the dogs brought by the Basques were simply Australian herding dogs of British collie type. According to Clel Georgetta, a sheep and cattle rancher who later became a lawyer and member of the Nevada legislature, these dogs were "brought over from Australia. Some call them American shepherd, but the right name for the breed is border collie because they came [originally] from the south part of Scotland." (*Kelley of the Triune, Biography of a Sheep Dog* by Clel Georgetta, 1979 Venture Publishing, Reno, Nevada). Whatever the case, the breed developed in the American West and is still a popular breed on western sheep ranches.

The modern Australian Shepherd is a slightly larger dog than the Border Collie with a naturally short or docked tail. Some are born with a tail, which their owners or breeders may leave long, making these dogs

An Australian Shepherd works Barbados sheep at a herding clinic.

virtually indistinguishable from a Border Collie on looks alone, although they may have a more blocky head and their working style is somewhat different. Blue and red merle are typical colors, but black-and-white or red-and-white are also seen, all of which may have tan markings. It is an all-around working breed, able to handle all types of stock, and does well

Smooth-coated Border Collies are less popular in the United States today, but you still see them. Missi belongs to Rebecca and Joseph Mayer of East Ryegate, Vermont.

at a variety of sports. It is recognized and registered by the American Kennel Club, although it also has its own breed club and registry, the Australian Shepherd Club of America.

THE MCNAB

The McNab is possibly the most interesting and least known of the American herding breeds. It developed from working collies imported from Scotland in the late 19th century by Alexander McNab, a sheep rancher in Northern California. The Mendocino Valley consists of dry, steep mountain slopes, which are hot in the summer, and abundantly accented with foxtails and burrs. Because of the climate and geography of the countryside where he lived, McNab imported mostly smooth-coated dogs from his native country. The breed that developed from these dogs is medium-sized, black-and-white, smooth-coated and prick-

Zak, a smooth-coated, prick-eared Border Collie, belongs to Chuck and Beth Lyons of Ithaca, New York.

eared. McNabs are considered more direct and forceful on stock than the Border Collie, and a protective, one-man or one-family dog. They are still favored by Northern California sheep and cattle ranchers, but are rare elsewhere in the country. They are registered by the National Stock Dog Registry, which will register herding dogs of any breed, including Australian Shepherds and Border Collies.

These four breeds of herding dog are directly related to the Border Collie—his cousins. They are descended from the old working collies of the last century and have been developed on American soil. As we have seen, Border Collies either came from the same or similar stock imported into the United States in the 18th and 19th centuries, or developed from that same stock in Britain and Ireland and subsequently imported to the United States.

Border Collie Registries and Trials

Unlike Britain, which has four separate countries competing in sheepdog trials but only one registry for the working Border Collie, the International Sheep Dog Society (ISDS), there are three registries for Border Collies alone in the United States—the North American Sheep Dog Society (NASDS), which is the oldest, the American International Border Collie Registry (AIBC), and the American Border Collie Association, Inc. (ABCA), which is the most recently formed of the three. These registries have played a major role in the history of the breed in this country. Other registries record Border Collies, but they are multi-breed registries, and will be considered later. [Note: numbers that follow a dog's name are their ISDS registration number unless preceded by "NA" (an NASDS registration), "AIBC" (which is self explanatory), or "ABC" (an ABCA registration). NR means a dog is not registered.]

THE NORTH AMERICAN SHEEP DOG SOCIETY (NASDS)

Prior to World War II, American Border Collies were registered with the International Sheep Dog Society (ISDS) in Britain. James Reid, secretary of ISDS for more than 32 years, beginning in 1913, was also instrumental in forming the North American Sheep Dog Society, and guiding its early years. Founded in 1940, NASDS had among its charter members, or those joining it while it was still in the fledgling stage—Sam Stoddart, Luke Pasco, Carl Bradford, Sr., Carroll Shaffner, Arthur Allen, and other prominent American sheepdog handlers of the day. Dr. Donald Bell of Wooster, Ohio became the first secretary, and in 1942, NASDS or "the North American," as it is commonly known, began registering American-bred dogs. Many of the dogs of the day were imported along with their ISDS registration numbers, and then also registered by NASDS. Sam Stoddart's Spot 308 posthumously became NA1, and, as was the custom, would have appeared in pedigrees as "Stoddart's Imp. Spot 1 (308)." Arthur Allen became president in 1951 and remained at the helm until his death in 1997. NASDS sponsors the North American Supreme Championship Trials, which were held every year, but are no longer held annually.

A Border Collie, herding sheep at a sheepdog trial in New England.

THE AMERICAN INTERNATIONAL BORDER COLLIE REGISTRY (AIBC)

In 1951, a disagreement arose among the prominent members of NASDS and certain of them were ousted from leadership roles. These men formed the Iowa Border Collie Association, from which the American International Border Collie Registry developed in 1952. Olive Downs of Ames, Iowa was the first secretary, her husband, Millard E. Downs, was the first treasurer, and Dewey Jontz was the first president.

AIBC was incorporated in Iowa and, like NASDS before it, became an affiliate member of ISDS. The reason it was called "American International" and not just "American" was two-fold: first, the founders wanted to indicate their affiliation with ISDS, and second, the name "American Border Collie" was taken at the time by Ohio Border Collie breeder Howard McClain for a private registry for dogs of his own breeding, known as ABC or simply "McClain's". Other private registries also existed at the time, including "Topliff's" and "Perrot's", which was called the Border Collie Registry Bureau and would have appeared on pedigrees as BCRB. Eventually, these became absorbed by AIBC. There were also numerous desertions from NASDS to AIBC, the most notable being the mass defection in 1958 of Ray Parker and thirty other Border Collie breeders from Texas.

Olive Downs remained the secretary of AIBC until her retirement in 1964, when Ara Jontz, the wife of Dewey, took over. She did not remain secretary long, however, as she became ill and subsequently passed away, and the stud book passed to Jack Kaster in 1966. Jack Kaster maintained the stud book until only recently. Recently, it was passed to Sennette Parker of Chappell Hills, Texas, widow of the late Clifford Parker, a well-known handler.

THE AMERICAN BORDER COLLIE ASSOCIATION, INC. (ABCA)

In 1983, a group of about twenty sheepdog trial handlers met in Starkville, Mississippi, and started a third Border Collie registry, the American Border Collie Association. It, too, became an affiliate of ISDS. (Foreign registries wishing to become associated with ISDS pay an "affiliation fee", and ISDS considers such a collaboration to forge "a closer bond" and enables the organizations to "work more closely together for the benefit of the Border Collie." (Philip Hendry, secretary of ISDS, in a letter to ABCA on 28 January 1983)). Ralph Pulfer of Quincy, Ohio was the first president of ABCA, followed by Herbert Holmes of Sheffield, Texas.

Today, ABCA is the most active American Border Collie registry and registers the most dogs. It accepts registrations from ISDS and the other two American registries, provides a five-generation pedigree and has gone the furthest of the three in promoting the health of the breed, by listing eye and hip certifications on pedigrees when available. Its members, which secretary Patty Rogers says numbers 6,000, vote annually for a Board of Directors, the only Border Collie registry in America today to actually hold elections.

Some do not see the three registries in the U.S.A. as being rivals (apparently ISDS does not, since it has accepted affiliation with all three) but as serving differing needs or regions. However, both AIBC and ABCA were born in controversy, and each registry serves people from all over the country today. Having three registries tends to emphasize, if not promote, a splintering of factions. This was particularly noticeable recently when the American Kennel Club accepted the Border Collie for full recognition.

REGISTRATION IN CANADA

The situation in Canada is a bit different from the United States. In the U.S.A., concerns over whether dogs are purebred or not are not regulated by the government. In Canada, however, there is an Animal Pedigree Act (APA) regulated by the Ministry of Agriculture. Under this law, only one breed organization or registry may represent that breed, and the Minister of Agriculture must "be satisfied that the formation of [the] association to represent a breed is beneficial to the breeders of that breed and to the public at large." Furthermore, once Agriculture recognizes an organization, only dogs registered by that organization may be sold as "registered in Canada." It may be reasonable to assume that this is a protection for both buyers and sellers.

Up until 1992, Canadian Border Collie owners could register their dogs with one of the Border Collie registries in the U.S.A. The CKC, like the AKC, had a "Miscellaneous Class" in which the Border Collie and other "unrecognized breeds" could compete in events other than conformation. However, in August 1992, the CKC voted to officially recognize these breeds and eliminate the Miscellaneous Class. It passed a motion giving Border Collie owners until 1995 to form a national club and until 1996 to make recommendations to the CKC for participation in CKC conformation events, provided that Border Collie owners voted to accept the CKC as their breed representative. In December 1992 Border Collie owners and breeders were asked to complete a survey by the Ministry of Agriculture selecting an option for the breed. If Option 1 was the choice, Border Collie owners would continue to register in the United States and would no longer be able to continue to participate in CKC events. Their dogs would not be considered "Canadian-registered dogs."

If Option 2 was chosen, owners would form their own association and their dogs would be Canadian registered, but, because CKC voted to eliminate the Miscellaneous Class, Border Collies would no longer be eligible to participate in CKC activities. Option 3, to register with CKC, was the only choice that allowed Border Collies to participate in CKC activities.

The ballots were counted in March 1993, and Border Collie owners and breeders overwhelmingly voted for Option 2, to form their own Canadian Border Collie registry. The American Border Collie Association-Canada (ABCA-Canada) was approved for incorporation under the APA on August 26, 1994. It is directly affiliated with ABCA in the United States.

Martha McHardy and MarCar's Rogue negotiate a "Maltese cross" during a trial. He is an all-around dog that has earned Canadian Kennel Club CDX and Open Stock Dog titles, and is a North American Flyball Association champion.

EARLY SHEEPDOG TRIALS IN THE UNITED STATES

In 1880, a herding trial was held in Philadelphia called the "great International Collie Trial". It is considered by most to be the first sheepdog trial held in the United States. The dogs that competed in it were called simply "collies" or "Scotch collies." Some may have been the earliest show collies, somewhat different in looks from the working collie stock from which they developed, but still retaining some herding instincts. Others were simply working collies and may have been the ancestors of old-fashioned farm collies, English Shepherds, and Border Collies in this country. Several Philadelphia newspapers reported on this trial and the dogs that competed in it. One dog that particularly stood out was "Oscar," a "large black-and-tan collie." Oscar was bred by a Mr. Steel of Burnhead, Scotland and was reputed to have won "First Prize for penning sheep at the great show at Ayr, Scotland in 1876." He was imported by T.S. Cooper, a prominent importer of collies. That he still had herding ability was apparent, and one account has it that he won the trial. Another account mentions that "Tom," known as the "Philadelphia dog by reason of his long service in driving sheep from the stockyards [in Philadelphia] through the city to the Camden ferries," won the trial for his owner and handler, a drover, Mr. Charles Pugh.

Several other dogs were mentioned—"Lad", a smooth-coated tricolored dog owned by George Taylor of Sheffield, England; "Tweed," owned by Dr. J. W. Downey of New Market, Maryland and worked by a Mr. Phebus; "Fan," a tricolored bitch owned by T. S. Cooper and worked by a shepherd; "Lady Scotland," a tawny-red puppy, only six months old; and so on. What is remarkable about the accounts of this trial, at a time when bench shows were the vogue, is that very little space is taken up describing what the dogs look like, so we will never really know for sure. A great deal is made of their working style and ability to handle the sheep. The course was horseshoe-shaped, about 700 yards long, and tested only driving and penning skills. The handler was allowed to accompany the dog the entire way and could go either in front of or behind the sheep, showing that the working styles of the dogs were expected to be as diverse as their looks. In penning, a dog was permitted to bark. Mrs. Olive Downs, the first secretary of the American International Border Collie Registry said, this trial was "inspired by James Scott of Scotland, who had brought a ship load of sheep and cattle to America, and even sold the dogs he brought along." (From a letter written to Jane Porter of Greenacres, Washington, November 9, 1961.)

Accounts of other sheepdog trials began to appear in newspapers before or just at the turn of the century. One was held at the Vermont State Fair in 1908. The contestants described were two sables, a smooth-coated, a black-and-white collie, and a Bearded Collie named Miller's Bruce. Again, emphasis was on working ability. "Dash" and "eye" were considered important, as were patience and quiet style. This trial was set up similarly to British trials, with an outrun and fetch, a drive, and finally a pen. The reporter concluded that, "there is every hope that this interesting and instructive work will become popular at the State Fairs and open air shows of the future."

Trials did eventually catch on in America. Trials began to be held throughout the country at all the important agricultural fairs, at a variety of livestock events, and at Scottish games. As in Britain, many of the trials in turn spawned local and national associations that then took over organizing annual events. Writing about the importance of sheepdog trials in America, Luke Pasco, a well-known sheepdog handler and breeder from Massachusetts from the 1930s, said,

"Competitive Dog Trials started some eighty years ago and have really been the making of what the Border Collie is today. It has eliminated all the counterfeits. To this day our trials are perhaps one of the most important angles of the [sheep] dog industry. The course of our trials is such that any dog capable of going the course is likely to be a high class practical dog for any condition or type of farm or ranch work." (*Heather Jean, The Working Sheep Dog* by Luke Pasco, Sheep Breeder Inc., 1937.)

Arthur Allen, another notable Border Collie handler and breeder,

Among the competitors at the Canadian Open at Bond Head, Ontario, were some very well-known triallists from all over the USA and Canada. Seen here were the top 25 finalists and judge Charlie Relph from Keswick, England.

attributed the surge of interest in sheepdog trials in the 1920s to an increase in livestock importation and a new popularity of livestock shows and state fairs. He says,

"[The '20s saw a] new beginning of trials in the U.S., particularly in the Midwest. However, by 1930, the larger trials had shifted to the Eastern states. By 1940, the major trials were for the most part in the Midwest and far west. Competition was mostly singles. There were a few outstanding brace teams at trials and exhibitions in the forties. The last officially sanctioned brace trials were in 1970 and 1971 in Illinois.

"In the seventies, trials were well scattered over most of the U.S. hampered greatly by the high cost of travel and distance, along with the major problem of lack of unity and uniform trial rules, and one governing body that could resolve all matters of importance as they do in the British Isles." (*A Lifetime With The Working Collie* by Arthur Allen, 1979.)

Also at odds was the confusing variety of awards presented at different trials. Pasco's Jean, for example, was the "American Outdoor Champion" of 1932 and 1933, and the "American Indoor Champion" in 1933! Titles were spoken of without mention of the trial at which they were won as if they were national titles won at a trial that culminated the entire season, which was not necessarily the case. However, a number of trials eventually emerged that were universally accepted as prestigious. Among them were the Far Western International Sheep Dog Trials which ran from 1939 through 1964, the North American Supreme Championship sponsored by NASDS, the Canadian Open, the Midwest (held at Lodi, Ohio) and the Blue Grass National Open, held at Walnut Hill Farm in Lexington, Kentucky, from the 1960s through 1983.

AMERICAN BORDER COLLIES AND THEIR LEGENDARY HANDLERS

Registered Border Collies (though they were still called sheepdogs) began being imported into the United States soon after the International Sheep Dog Society (ISDS) was formed in 1906, but the dog considered to be the first significant import was Spot 308. Spot was bred by G. P. Brown of Berwickshire, England, and was born in 1920. He won his first trial in 1921, the International Shepherd's Cup in 1922, and became International Supreme Champion in 1923. He had a tremendous influence on the breed in Britain, Australia and the United States. In 1923 when he was three, he was sold to Sam Stoddart, a Scottish shepherd living and working in the United States. Stoddart was one of the leading breeders of registered Border Collies in America in the 1920s and '30s. He gave sheepdog demonstrations at agricultural fairs, and many of the early sheepdog handlers were introduced to the breed by seeing him there. He is considered by many to be the founder of the North American Sheep Dog Society, and Spot 308 became NA #1 posthumously.

Don Bell, the first secretary of NASDS, believed Spot had a considerable impact on the American Border Collie:

"Descendants of the renowned Spot symbolize the influence 'Old Spot' had on the quality of the good registered dogs in North America. It is significant that one rarely finds an outstanding American-bred registered dog which does not carry some of the 'blood' of Old Spot. What Britain gave up we gained, and it is proper to pay tribute to the founding sire of the registered Border Collies in North America." (*The Sheepman*, February, 1945.)

Preston Davonport, a shepherd from Massachusetts and a familiar figure at sheepdog trials in New England, also believed that Spot 308 was a pivotal force on sheepdog handlers in this country. He described the effect Sam Stoddart had on the early handlers,

"It was on [a] trip to the Brockton Massachusetts Fair with our flock of Southdowns that I bought my first Border Collie. I was intrigued with the incomparable working exhibition of Mr. Sam Stoddart and his dog, Spot.

"Spot became my ideal of a Border Collie. He was a larger than average dog, rough coated, black with white points, and an eye that was forever on a sheep. The handlers that were the principles of those early years were surely unanimous in their support of Sam Stoddart as the man who generated all the enthusiasm. It was Sam who pioneered the Border Collie interest." (*Northeastern Sheepdog Newsletter*, 1979 and 1980.)

A number of prominent breeders of the time began to perpetuate Spot's influence by breeding his progeny. There followed in the wake of Stoddart and Spot a great interest in sheepdog trialling among sheepmen and agriculturalists in the United States, though some men preferred giving demonstrations at fairs and rodeos, where they could meet farmers and ranchers face to face and promote the breed. Nancy Keller, a Border Collie archivist from Corydon, Indiana writes,

"Herding exhibitions were very significant in the development of the Border Collie in the United States after World War I. At that time the skill of using a Border Collie to work sheep was known to very few in this country, mostly hired shepherds or sheep breeders. Sheepdog trials were almost nonexistent, so the only exposure the majority of the public had to the Border Collie during that period was through herding demonstrations given at fairs and livestock exhibitions." (*The Shepherd's Dogge*, March 1989.)

If the desired effect was to publicize the breed, the audience reached was even broader for handlers whose Border Collies appeared in motion pictures. It was not at all unusual for experienced handlers to go to work for movie producers. Walt Disney made a number of films that had Border Collies in them. Charles Null's King, a smooth-coated American-bred dog that won the Far Western International Sheep Dog Trials for seven consecutive years from 1954 to 1960 and was extensively used in exhibitions, appeared in two movies, *Wild is the Wind* and *The Proud Rebel*. Another King, AIBC 777 belonging to Clint Harlow of Llano, Texas, also appeared in films, and Harlow trained him to work sheep with a monkey

Sheepdog trials have existed in the USA since the turn of the century. A Border Collie's true worth can be measured at such an event.

riding in a saddle on his back. A photo of him herding sheep with his monkey at the L.B.J. Ranch in Texas appeared shortly after Lyndon Johnson became President in 1964. Tricks of this sort were not considered undignified in those days, and certainly attracted attention to the breed.

Arthur Allen from McLeansboro, Illinois became a very well-known sheepdog trialist. His Imported Rock 7222, the 1954 North American Supreme Champion, was a son of Gilchrist's Spot 7320 and grandson of Wilson's Moss 5176. Rock appeared in two Walt Disney movies, *Border Collies in Action* and *Arizona Sheep Dog*, the latter staring Allen's little black

Border Collie, Nickey NA2339, who all by himself shepherds five stray sheep through the Arizona wilderness to rejoin the flock, demonstrating a Border Collie's great skill. Allen's imported dogs won every North American Supreme (the trial sponsored by NASDS) from 1954 through 1976, including twenty-one consecutive years. He imported and bred many Border Collies from outstanding British lines that had a marked effect on the breed in the United States, particularly in the early years.

Jim Shearer from Pennsylvania also worked for Walt Disney. His Tim, sired by Imported Rock, is probably the Border Collie that appeared in the Disney film, *101 Tasks of Hercules.* Shearer considered Tim his best dog ever and said that when working on a ranch in California that "included 42,000 acres of different terrain and all kinds of situations, [Tim] proved himself an indefatigable worker and companion." As a demonstration of Tim's skill, Shearer mentions "gathering 2000 wild Santa Barbara sheep for shipping to market."

In order to understand the background of the modern Border Collie in America, we must consider how very involved in the agricultural industry the major breeders and trialists of this period were. Many of them were farmers, ranchers, hired shepherds, farm managers, or worked in livestock research or education at the agricultural schools of large universities. This made for someone familiar with breeding and genetics who could comprehend the needs of the industry and grasp what traits to look for in a good herding dog. At the same time as Border Collies were being imported from Britain to become the foundation stock of the breed in this country, their American-bred progeny were also making their mark.

Carl Bradford worked at the sheep facility at the Ohio Agricultural Research and Development Center and went on to become active in exhibitions and demonstrations beginning in the mid-1940s. He may be credited with exposing hundreds of farmers to the working abilities of the Border Collie. All of his dogs were American-bred until 1942, when he imported Towser 5324, a grandson of J.M. Wilson's Cap 3036 and Tess 7561, a daughter of Hislop's Sweep 3834. Towser and Tess were the paternal great-grandparents of Dick and Ada Karrasch's Mississinewa Prince Val UDT NA101132. Val, says Keller, "was the first significant American Border Collie obedience winner, [and] in addition to his obedience career he was a fine herding dog who was used in a number of exhibitions."

Other important dogs of Carl Bradford's were Roy 11464, the sire of Lewis Pence's Rick NA10113, who won the Bluegrass Sheepdog Trial in 1966 and is featured in a number of working and obedience lines; and Spot 21963, imported by Harold Miller of Kentucky, who had the starring role in the movie *Mountain Born*, a full-brother to Tot Longton's Rob 21959 and half-brother to John Gilchrist's famous Spot 24981.

Carroll Shaffner, from Central Illinois, worked as a shepherd in Ohio and finally at Pennsylvania State University, where in 1950 he acquired his first imported Border Collie, Roy 5323, purchased from Jim Shearer. Subsequently, Shaffner imported his own stud dogs every year from Scotland, many of which were bred by the well-known Scottish trialer, John Purdie. Many American Border Collies, particularly in the East and Midwest, still have Shaffner-bred dogs in their pedigrees.

Triallist Ada Karrasch, penning at the Canadian Open at Bond Head, Ontario.

The '60s, '70s and '80s saw Pope Robertson of Texas as one of the top American Border Collie trainers and trialers. His American-bred Lash AIBC 892 became the first dog to win the Kentucky Bluegrass Open in 1963. Lash was the son of imported Mirk II 15297, who was a full-brother to Bathgate's Meg 12848 and a half-brother to Fraser's Mindrum Cap 14915, the 1960 English Driving Champion, and to Longton's Nell 12462. Foss 9538, Lash's dam, was a granddaughter of 1948 Welsh National Champion Jaff 4313.

Lash founded a line of Texas herding trial dogs. He sired Robertson's Lash II AIBC 3755, who won the Bluegrass Open in 1967; and many of his progeny were Texas Dogs of the Year, an important award. Lash's line survives today through many modern Texas trial dogs.

Lewis Pence was another American handler who was among the first to train his own trialling dogs. He effectively demonstrated his training methods in the many successful herding clinics he taught throughout this country. He believed in training with kindness and consistent firmness when many other handlers used forceful methods. A number of young handlers who later went on to make a name for themselves in the trialing world were protegés of Pence. Foremost among these was Bruce Fogt.

Today in America women compete on equal footing with men in sheepdog trials, but it was not always so. In the early days of trialling in the U.S.A., women competed in a class of their own at sheepdog trials. Ada Karrasch, whose connection with Mississinewa Prince Val is known, was the first modern woman handler to compete successfully with men in American sheepdog trials, beginning in the 1960s. The Karrasches owned and operated a turkey-breeding farm in Indiana. Val was bought for and originally trained to move the turkeys about the farm as needed to ensure economic success. He enabled Ada to gather eggs without fear of being attacked by the turkeys. Later, Val was campaigned in both obedience and sheepdog trials. Ada and her husband Dick made a lasting contribution to both herding and obedience through their participation in both types of competitive sporting events, and by training dogs for both competitions. "There has always been somewhat of an adversarial

Triallist Ralph Pulfer from Ohio, penning at the Canadian Open.

relationship between herding people and obedience Border Collie people," says Nancy Keller. "Dick and Ada helped bridge that gap."

If it could be said that there is another gap between the early legendary trialers and the handlers of today, the Pulfer brothers of Ohio may have helped to bridge that gap. Ralph Pulfer has been one of the most victorious sheepdog trial handlers in North America. He has imported over a hundred dogs from Scotland, and all of his top-winning trial dogs were imported. Dogs of note were Rory, Dan, Ken, and Clint. His Nap won the 1992 Purina Award for the Outstanding Field Trial Herding Dog, for points accumulated in the top five places in as many as 36 trials in one year. (This award has been given by the Ralston Purina Company since 1988.) His Imp. Shep 112791 was the sire of Bill Berhow's Nick ABC1778.

Imported red-and-white Dell, owned by Lewis Pulfer, had a big influence on the American Border Collie. Seen here showing her style at a trial.

Ralph's brother, Lewis Pulfer, has also been a top trial handler, and his imported Dell 96946, a red-and-white bitch with great style, has had as much an influence on the modern breed as many an imported sire. She was a daughter of McConnel's Moss 77473 and Brownlie's Fly 74537. She was imported in 1980, in whelp to Lewis Pulfer's Craig 106113 (imported at the same time), and she won a trial for Pulfer only two weeks after her arrival in the U.S.A. In that year she had five trial wins for Pulfer and she produced progeny that lived up to her reputation. She was the dam or granddam of some of the most important trialing dogs in America today, including Bruce Fogt's Hope AIBC36007 and Dodie Green's Soot ABC12218. There are numerous accounts of this kind about illustrious American sheepdog handlers and their outstanding dogs, and little room to tell them.

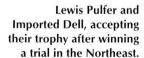

Lewis Pulfer and Imported Dell, accepting their trophy after winning a trial in the Northeast.

THE BORDER COLLIE IN CANADA

The history of the Border Collie in Canada may be said to parallel that in the United States, but there are some differences. In the early 1800s, before Canada was an independent country, the Hudson's Bay Company (HBC) promoted the sheep industry in order to have a readily available supply of mutton and wool for colonists and their own employees. At their prompting, many shepherds from Great Britain migrated to British Columbia to tend the flocks on the island of Vancouver, where the rolling hills and moderate sea climate were similar to what they knew. This area still supports large commercial sheep operations. Further east, in the plains provinces of Saskatchewan and Alberta, there are still many large sheep and cattle ranches, and Canada still has vast tracts of forested wilderness areas. Ranching has been the main focus of Border Collie breeding in this part of Canada in the past, with trials taking on only a minor role. According to Richard Tipton of Lone Pine, Alberta, Border Collies that were introduced into western Canada in the 1800s and early 1900s were used on cattle and sheep ranches and more or less bred to extinction by crossbreeding with other types of dogs. It was he and several other breeder/ranchers that re-introduced the Border Collie to western Canada by judicious breeding and importation. Indeed, some consider Richard Tipton to be the "grandfather of trialing and breeding" in Alberta, and today, due to the influence of Tipton and others, trialing has become more important. Tipton's Robbie, the son of a bitch he imported from Jack Knox in the United States, has had a big influence on Border Collies in Alberta and Saskatchewan.

Other breeders of note in western Canada are: John Wickson of Courtenay, British Columbia, who has been breeding, training and trialling for decades, and now in his twilight years still gives active sheepdog demonstrations; "Scotty" Steward of Campbell River, British Columbia, who imported a bitch named Dot in whelp to the 1975 and 1979 International Supreme Champion, McPherson's Zac 66166, and many other top Canadian dogs; Elvin Kop of Westerose, Alberta, whose key dogs, Jeff and Bliss, have had a big influence on the breed in Canada; Peter Gonnett of Broderick, Saskatchewan, whose key dog, Craig, came in twelfth overall at the 1995 USBCHA National Finals; Dale Montgomery of Maple Creek, Saskatchewan, whose dog, Huck, is a top sire of many western Canadian working and trial dogs; and so on.

In eastern Canada, where farms are smaller and more similar to those in the eastern United States, there have been more trials and more exchange among handlers from both sides of the border, and between those in Canada and Great Britain. Particularly from Ontario, several names come to mind as having influenced the breed: Jim Clark, Bill McMichael, and Alex McKinvin.

Triallist Jack Knox and his Imported Dryden Craig, stepping onto the course at the 1979 Canadian Open.

The Border Collie
in America Today

SHEEPDOG TRIALS IN THE U.S.A. TODAY

As the larger-than-life handlers began to retire or pass away, a new breed of handler began to take their place. The sheepdog handlers of yesteryear worked in agriculture and used Border Collies to help them in their jobs. Though some of today's trial handlers farm for a living, many are only involved with Border Collies in the sport of trialling. Some keep a few sheep just to train their dogs, some keep no sheep at all but travel to train their dogs. Some are "professional handlers"—they make their living from the Border Collie, breeding and selling puppies, traveling the "sheepdog trial circuit," taking home prize money, getting paid to judge trials, teaching herding and judging clinics, or giving private lessons to would-be handlers.

While most trials in America today follow a British format, Americans have experimented with a variety of trial schemes. The use of a "drop pen", instead of a dog and handler to hold the sheep at the top of an outrun, was in vogue at some trials a few years ago. Basically, it was a pen with an ordinary gate at the back and a top-pivoting gate at the front. The sheep for each run were placed in the pen through the back gate, and someone held a long rope behind the pen that was attached to and operated the front gate. When the competing dog came up behind the pen on his outrun, the person holding the rope lifted the gate, and the dog drove the sheep out of the pen (the lift). The run then proceeded as usual. This didn't always work as imagined. Some dogs were spooked by the lifting of the gate, or did not recognize sheep in the pen as being the ones to be lifted. But it did free up all handlers and dogs so they could run in the trial. It is not used much today, if at all. Bridges, chutes or Maltese crosses have also been used instead of drive panels.

A point system for judging was devised in the 1970s and used at some trials through the early 1980s. Instead of starting a run with a given number of points and having points deducted for gates missed, stopping, and errors of style, a dog began each run with no points and gained points for the number of sheep that went through each set of panels. Retries of

A "drop pen" is used at a trial in the Northeast. Note that the dog is in place behind the pen and the gate has been lifted to release the sheep.

each section of the course were allowed in an attempt to "get the job done."

While there are still some trials that use this system, most have returned to the British method. Some trials today use an aggregate scoring method— the dogs that score highest the first day also run the second day, and the two scores are combined to determine the winner. Length of outruns, time allotments, number of sheep for each run, and the inclusion or exclusion of particular maneuvers may also vary from trial to trial.

Equally confusing will be the definitions of the classes in trials in America. The Open Class is almost always for experienced dogs and handlers. A Novice Trial or class is usually for inexperienced handlers and dogs, but in some parts of the country this is called Ranch Class or Novice-Novice. A Pro-Novice would be for veteran handlers with untried dogs, but may be referred to as an Open Ranch in some parts of the country. The United States Border Collie Handlers Association (USBCHA) describes the Open Ranch as being for *all* handlers with inexperienced dogs *or* for inexperienced handlers with experienced dogs. One more class must be mentioned: the Nursery Class. This is the only one with an age limit (for dogs) attached, and it is for young dogs, however, a few trials crop up where the Novice Class is called Nursery Class.

A "bridge," one of the varying examples of an obstacle used in an American trial.

We will not go into a description of the courses involved in each of these classes of trial because, although some standardization has been achieved throughout the country due to the efforts of USBCHA, there are still myriad trials that are run strictly by local rules.

Trials are run today at every imaginable event, from county agricultural fairs to rodeos, and many stand alone as events in their own right. Trials in different parts of the country might have longer or shorter outruns, depending on what dogs in that part of the country are used to. For example, in New England, where farms and fields are small, trials usually have short outruns. Dogs worked under these conditions often do not do as well competing with dogs from other parts of the country where the dogs are used to long outruns. Those that do excel attest to the training skills of their handler. "Arena" trials are popular in some areas—trials held in covered livestock arenas or on racetracks.

As with the earlier trials, some trials have emerged today that are

An indoor "arena trial" held in Fryeburg, Maine.

considered important. Bear in mind that the trial situation in this country is a fluid one, and trials that are enormously popular today and attract a large entry could be gone tomorrow when the group running it loses interest or a key instigator is removed from the scene. In 1990, the Kentucky Bluegrass National Open was revived, this time in Louisville, and regained prestige. The North American Supreme is still put on by NASDS, but with less regularity. The North American International Livestock Exposition Sheepdog Trial began in 1991 and is held in November at the Kentucky State Fair Exposition Center in Louisville, attracting a large entry from all over the country and Canada. The Triple Crown of Virginia, held in May, has become an important trial in recent years. It is actually three trials in one, held over a nine-day period—the Blue Ridge Open, sponsored by Hill's Science Diet and held at Ethel Conrad's farm in White Post; the Seclusival Open, sponsored by Joy Dog Food and held at Stu and Linda Ligon's farm in Shipman; and the Oatlands Open, sponsored by Purina Dog Food and held in Leesburg. USBCHA holds its National Finals in September, including an open and nursery trial, and is considered by most handlers to be a culmination of the trialling year. In various parts of the country, other long-running trials have become prestigious—the World Sheepdog Championship in Meeker, Colorado, the SAILA (Southern Arizona International Livestock Association) Open in Arizona, the Heart of Dixie Open in Alabama, and the Southern California Master's Cup Sheep Dog Trial, to name a few. Many of these trials have large purses attached to them, making them more attractive to handlers.

Trainer Bruce Fogt, emphasizing a point at a herding clinic in the Northeast.

Trials are still the single most important influence on the Border Collie in this country, since it is still from trial dogs that most of the breeding stock descends. Trials are at an all-time high in popularity and there is a great interest in Border Collies. People who may have at one time had Border Collies simply as companions or for obedience are now interested in them as working dogs and have become amateur trialers. Some people are even willing to pay large sums to professionals to teach them how to train their dogs, larger sums to have professionals train their dogs for them, and yet larger amounts to purchase a fully trained and already trial-winning dog. So, while modern sheepdog trials have become more of a highly competitive sport, we have used it here to introduce the dogs and handlers that had the biggest effect on the breed today.

Above: Locally bred Lyn belongs to Suzanne West of Oliver Springs, Tennessee. Note her beautiful curly coat and the white stripe down her back! *Below:* A very small outdoor course at one of the local "arena trials" in the Northeast. Many of these very small trials have been discontinued or remain only to demonstrate herding in a public venue.

TODAY'S DOGS AND HANDLERS

While Spot 308, Wiston Cap and the Gilchrists' Spots continue to have some influence on the American Border Collie, new lines have in recent years come to the fore in American Collie pedigrees. Today the progeny of more current British trials winners have been the subject of importation to the United States. Names like Price's Davy 131049, Jones' Mac 116944 (the so-called "Butcher's Dog"), Longton's Bess 101142, and Bwlch Taff 113248 appear most frequently in the pedigrees of modern American dogs, with the names of Welsh dogs seeming to predominate today where once it was Scottish or northern English dogs. Perhaps it is as true in Britain and Ireland as here in the U.S.A., but some dogs are ever popular as sires, while others, even if they are National or International Champions, hardly ever seem to get used at stud.

"It is an unfortunate tendency among trial people in this country," says Nancy Keller, "to import one generation of dogs for trialling, breed stock dogs from them, and then obtain the next generation of trial dogs from overseas instead of training dogs of their own breeding. How many potentially top lines are fading into oblivion because breeders seek out the imports instead of American-bred dogs?" The question is well taken. However, there are a number of American lines where the significance of imported dogs has been less important. These lines appear mostly in the pedigrees of farm and ranch dogs or dogs working the local trial circuits. Now that trials are more popular, these lines are beginning to have more impact on the important trial dogs in the United States.

There are a number of dogs and handlers in America that come to mind as significant. Bill Berhow's American-bred Nick ABC1778 is one. A son of Ralph Pulfer's Shep 112791 and Nan 126698, Nick was the 1990 and '91 winner of the Purina Award for Outstanding Field Trial Herding Dog and the 1989, '90 and '93 USBCHA National Finals winner. Two others are Bruce Fogt's Hope AIBC36007 and Molly ABC7747. Hope, a daughter of Pulfer's Dell, was conceived in Scotland but born in the United States. She was 1988 winner of the Purina Award and the USBCHA National Finals Winner in 1987. Molly, a daughter of Tommy Wilson's Roy ABC3455—himself a significant dog and winner of the 1989 Purina Award—was the 1992 USBCHA National Finals Winner. Bruce Fogt, like his mentor Lewis Pence, gives training clinics all over the country.

Others include Karen Thomason's Buttersett Lad 175393, a son of Thomas Longton's Tweed 140476, who has sired some very promising dogs including the 1995 winner of the USBCHA Nursery Trial; Dodie Green's Soot ABC12218, a granddaughter of Pulfer's Dell, who won the 1993 Purina Award; Herbert Holmes's Dave, a Guild's Tweed son; David Rogers's Collster Chip ABC273, a son of J. R. Thomas' Craig 59425; and Jack Knox's Ettrick line. Knox was a shepherd in the Ettrick Valley of Scotland before moving to the U.S.A. and establishing Ettrick Kennels. His imported Dryden Craig 80254 had a big influence on both trialling and obedience Border Collies in the '80s that continues through today. Knox's wife Kathy is also a successful trialist and breeder, and

Raine, daughter of a successful trial dog (Thomason's Butterset Lad), trials for her owner Suzanne West of Oliver Springs, Tennessee.

Knox himself has played an important role in shaping handlers by teaching herding clinics throughout the country. There are certainly others, but we haven't the room to mention them all here.

Today in America, there are trials in every area of the country, particularly during the summer months, when there is a trial just about every weekend, and some weekends show three or four. We are not speaking about local trials that perhaps ten or twenty handlers attend, but large two- or three-day events in which handlers from all over the country compete, with several different classes for fifty or more dogs!

Multi-breed Organizations that Register the Border Collie

THE AMERICAN KENNEL CLUB (AKC)

No book on the Border Collie in America today would be complete without a discussion of the relationship the Border Collie has had with the American Kennel Club, for that relationship has provided a major controversy that spans decades. Up until December 13, 1994, AKC did not register the breed. On that day, the Board of Directors of AKC voted to admit the Border Collie as a full participant in all their activities. Until that time, Border Collies had been able to participate only in AKC obedience and tracking events in the Miscellaneous Class with an Indefinite Listing Privilege number (ILP).

The Border Collie's history with the AKC, however, goes back many years. Officially, the AKC claims that the Border Collie was first associated with them in 1955 when the Miscellaneous Class was implemented. However, others claim that the Border Collie had been associated with AKC since obedience was sanctioned by AKC in the early 1930s.

It is unclear why this point is in dispute, but whatever the case, the Border Collie had been in the AKC Miscellaneous Class for quite a long time, and has been shown in the obedience ring for even longer. Just as there are particular working lines, there are lines of Border Collies that have been bred strictly for obedience for many years in the United States. It is no wonder that, when the AKC announced in 1994 that it would drop its Miscellaneous Class, people who had been showing their Border Collies in obedience for many years became alarmed. Furthermore, those with Border Collies in herding trials also became alarmed. To one group, it meant that the Border Collie might possibly be dropped altogether from the AKC and they would no longer be able to compete in obedience

A young pup is being trained: Tyche Total Recall ("Callie"), Gloria Smith's favorite dog. All grown up now, Callie is doing well in agility as well as herding.

with their dogs. To the other group, it meant that the AKC was making its move on the Border Collie, which to them spelled disaster—they felt the breed would change, losing its working abilities. Individuals and groups began to line up and take sides. New groups were formed and opinions flew.

In the end, despite pressure to the contrary, the AKC Board of Directors voted to admit the Border Collie with "all attendant privileges." Those "privileges" include entry into the Herding Group and participation in all AKC herding and agility events, effective February 1, 1995, and show classification in the Herding Group in breed or bench shows, effective October 1, 1995. The AKC standard for the Border Collie was approved January 10, 1995, effective April 30, 1995. It was published and

Callie enjoys cooling off in the kiddie pool after a vigorous game of ball.

may be seen in the March 1995 issue of the *Gazette,* the official magazine of the AKC.

Two clubs promoted recognition, the Border Collie Society of America (BCSA) and the American Border Collie Alliance (ABCA—the club). BCSA became the parent club for the Border Collie in the AKC. There

The enthusiastic Karim's Clio of Fortune, Am. & Mex. CD, CGC & Therapy Dog, owned by Linda Schulte, is herding Barbados sheep.

are still many individuals and some organizations actively opposing AKC registration, in particular the American Border Collie Association (ABCA—the registry) and the United States Border Collie Club (USBCC).

It is this author's opinion that AKC recognition does not necessarily spell disaster for the breed as a whole. Just as separate Border Collie obedience lines have developed alongside the working lines, it is likely that separate show lines will develop that may become different from the working lines, as they have in other working breeds. Already it can be seen that proponents of show Border Collies prefer a dog with a heavier coat and bone structure, a more closely coupled body and a shorter leg length. A dog built like that would not have the stamina, speed and maneuverability that a working dog requires. However, those who wish may still register their dogs with NASDS, AIBC, or ABCA and those people wanting working lines may still go to people breeding herding lines to get them. Even the obedience people still have a choice. Some take their responsibility to the working legacy of the breed seriously and are promoting an open or frequently opened stud book for the AKC Border Collie so that breeders may periodically breed back to working lines. If the stud book is eventually closed, some may obtain working stock in Britain and register them with the British Kennel Club, since the AKC will accept foreign registrations. Because there is still the United Kennel Club, which also holds obedience trials and matches (although fewer than AKC and farther between) and has been registering Border Collies for years, some obedience owners may not even register with the AKC.

These two beautiful dogs waiting for their turn at the sheep are Candlewind Dreamvalley Pete and Glen Car'n Dreamvalley Nicki, owned by Victoria Hayes of Cleveland, Ohio. Pete is a Therapy Dog that regularly gives public demonstrations in agility, herding and responsible dog ownership.

THE UNITED KENNEL CLUB (UKC)

The United Kennel Club was founded in 1898 to register purebred dogs. Other than the date, UKC does not distribute an official history. It considers itself a "working dog" registry because, since its inception it has "advocated that breeding for conformation alone can be a great disadvantage to a particular breed" and "breeders are encouraged to breed for the 'total dog'". To this end it publishes a code of ethics which, however, cannot be considered effective as it contains a disclaimer which states, "Inasmuch as a Code of Ethics is a guideline, not rules, regulations or legal documents, they do not carry an enforceable punishment." In this, it is no different from any other registry in the U.S.A.

UKC claims to register "approximately 212 different breeds of dogs." including the Border Collie, but in two separate correspondences with the UKC, this author was unable to obtain a history of the Border Collie with the registry. It claims that "the total number of Border Collies registered with the United Kennel Club is not available; we do not keep count of the number of dogs registered." In its favor, the UKC has long been registering many breeds that the AKC would not touch, did not consider purebred, or have just gotten around to recognizing. These breeds would not have otherwise had a registry or access to dog sports. Only recently, the UKC has joined with the American Mixed Breeds Obedience Registry (AMBOR) to afford owners of mixed breeds similar privileges.

The UKC sanctions conformation as well as obedience and agility events, with the Border Collie being eligible to enter the obedience and agility events. In personal correspondence with this author, it claimed that the "American Border Collie *Breed* Association has asked that the UKC not sponsor conformation events for the Border Collie" and that they will honor the request. Admirable, but, in as much as there is no American Border Collie Breed Association we can only guess that it must mean the American Border Collie Association, a registry, or the United States Border Collie Club, a club, neither of which represent the breed as a whole and both of which have been openly opposed to AKC recognition.

THE NATIONAL STOCK DOG REGISTRY (NSD)

The National Stock Dog Registry in Butler, Indiana was founded by E.G. Emanuel in the 1950s as a registry for English Shepherds, but, as we have seen, now registers working stock dogs of a variety of breeds, including the Border Collie. It also publishes a magazine, *The National Stock Dog*, sponsors stockdog trials, and as of September 1994, has had a "Working Stock Dog Program," which offers working degrees. The first of these degrees is in General Obedience and seems rather paltry. A dog must be able to heel, sit, down, stay and come, and the owner must have a written statement from a "qualified obedience instructor" that the dog is well trained in these areas. The second degree, Ranch, is a trialing award, but also seems vague and inadequate, requiring only that "the dog must find the livestock, gather the livestock, and move the livestock from one area to another within the required time limit in three different events." The Marketing Degree is somewhat different from awards given by other organizations and illustrates the NSD's foundation in commercial working stock, requiring the dog to pen and load livestock into a trailer or truck within a time limit and in three separate events. Finally, the Championship award requires a top three placing in three different trials having no less than 30 competitors each.

CLUBS AND ASSOCIATIONS

There are numerous Border Collie clubs throughout the country. Most are local herding organizations that put on local or regional trials and organize herding and judging clinics (workshops). Almost every state or region has one, and some of the larger states, like California, have two or more. A few include other herding breeds among their purview. For other sports, like obedience, agility and flyball, Border Collie owners associate with owners of other breeds in clubs that cater to the particular sport or join general dog training clubs.

As we have seen, there is no one registry for Border Collies in the United States, and the same has been true of a national breed club. To date there have been four national Border Collie clubs: the United States Border Collie Club (USBCC), the Border Collie Club of America (BCCA), the Border Collie Society of America (BCSA) and the American Border Collie Alliance (ABCA, which should not be confused with the registry that has the same initials). Only USBCC and BCSA still remain along with a national trial handlers association (USBCHA), and a separate, independent national Border Collie rescue organization (NABCRN).

This adorable pup, Jack, aged seven weeks, looks to its owner Donna Lumme for direction.

THE UNITED STATES BORDER COLLIE HANDLERS ASSOCIATION (USBCHA)

In 1979, a group of trial handlers got together and formed the United States Border Collie Handlers Association. Bob Childress of Texas was the first president and George Conboy of Indiana the first secretary. Other charter members were Jim Varnon of Texas, Wilbur Miller of Indiana, Ted Johnson of Alabama, Robert Barlow of Tennessee, Lewis Pulfer of Ohio, John Bauserman of Virginia, Walt Jagger of Pennsylvania, Tom Conn of Pennsylvania, and George Gould of Maine—a truly national

Karen Clanin of Atascadero, California trained all her obedience, tracking, and Schutzhund Border Collies on a variety of livestock. This is her Karim's Pinny, UDT at three months old, herding ducks.

roster of well-known handlers. USBCHA's by-laws state that "one of the express purposes of forming the Association was to set forth rules as to how the trials were to be conducted in the United States." To this end, USBCHA has a very long, impressive list of rules which include axioms on the humane treatment of dogs and livestock, regulations for competitors (including a dress code accompanied by a fine for failure to comply), and detailed rules to govern every aspect of running, and running in, a trial. Nathan Mooney is the president and Francis Raley the secretary of the 400-member association.

Clanin's dogs come from working stock and she prides herself on breeding dogs that work. This is her Karim's Mark, CD, herding pygmy goats.

USBCHA sponsors two culminating trials a year, an Open National Finals and a Nursery National Finals. Among past winners of the Open have been Jack Knox with Jed in 1979 and '80, Bruce Fogt with Hope in 1987 and Molly in 1992, and Bill Berhow with Nick in 1989, '90 and '93. Besides prestige and trophies, there are money awards, making it small wonder that entries run very high for the USBCHA National Finals. The 1995 USBCHA National Finals also points out how far women have come in this sport. There were 120 handler-and-dog teams entered in the three-day Open held in Wyoming in 1995, and the Grand Champion was Kathy Knox of Missouri with six-year-old Ettrick Bob ABC 63357.

Martha McHardy, an occupational therapist from Victoria, British Columbia, is one of the new breed of Border Collie handlers that does everything one can do with a dog, and does it well. Here she is seen with her key breeding male, Vic, a son of trial champion Berhow's Nick.

1995 was also the first year that a small contingent of Canadian handlers qualified and competed at the USBCHA National Finals, from which came 25% of the top qualifiers, an achievement indicative of the caliber of handlers and dogs from Canada. A Canadian woman took second place — Reserve Champions were Amanda Milliken and her six-year-old Canadian-bred Hazel.

THE NORTH AMERICAN BORDER COLLIE RESCUE NETWORK (NABCRN)
As we have seen, the Border Collie is becoming a popular breed in North America. As more and more people who do not understand the

breed acquire a Border Collie, we see increasing numbers of Border Collies in need of rescue each year.

Many people have been involved individuals or in local groups in Border Collie rescue, but when a large number of dogs are rescued, an area's resources can be strained or exhausted, and rescue volunteers must seek farther afield to find appropriate homes. Furthermore, many doing Border Collie rescue were suffering from "burn out" because of a paucity of resources for them to fall back on. In 1993, when a worst-case situation occurred, where people in one area of the country were called on to rescue over a hundred sheepdogs (Border Collies, Australian Shepherds, Kelpies, and their crosses) of all ages from a puppy mill whose owner became ill, there became a definite need for a national Border Collie rescue effort.

Martha McHardy's Vic with three of his sons MarCar's Styx, MarCar's Jack, and MarCar's Rogue. Rogue is McHardy's United States Border Collie Handlers Association National Nursery Qualifier and, she says, he "demonstrates the versatility and soundness that I desire in my breeding."

Since the Border Collie did not have a single national breed organization or registry that could assume the unification of rescue efforts, what seemed appropriate was an independently operating rescue effort to serve the needs of the Border Collie community at large, and ultimately to best serve the needs of the breed. Thus in January 1994 the North American Border Collie Rescue Network (NABCRN) was born.

NABCRN is a support network for members, providing resources to those who are doing Border Collie rescue in Canada and the United States. It publishes a newsletter, maintains a library of other rescue material and resources, and provides educational material to rescue people and the general public. Rescue volunteers provide a variety of services from simple referrals to retraining of dogs with severe behavioral problems. They may provide temporary homes for rescued dogs (foster care), permanent placement, veterinary evaluation and care, neutering or spaying before placement, evaluation of temperament and herding ability,

Jes, who belongs to Connie Jacobs of Helena, Montana, is a rescue dog that was tagged as a Border Collie-Aussie cross by the shelter. Since blue merle is common in Aussies and not so common in Borders, labeling like this is tempting when you don't really know.

counseling, education, and training to owners so that they may keep their dogs. The organization has maintained a rescue fund to cover extraordinary expenses incurred by rescue volunteers. To date, NABCRN has grown enormously, and it is beginning to see support from a variety of local and regional Border Collie organizations and some of the national Border Collie groups as well. Furthermore, it has spawned a number of other Border Collie rescue groups, some national and working through the Internet, and others that feel that working on a local level is more important and productive.

THE AMERICAN HERDING BREED ASSOCIATION (AHBA)

Before leaving this section, mention must be made of another organization that, while not devoted primarily to the Border Collie, has contributed some incentive toward the breed's duration in herding—the American Herding Breed Association. Founded in 1986 by three herding enthusiasts, Linda Rorem, Peggy Prater and Rita Carr, AHBA's goals were to provide herding breeds, and to encourage involvement in herding by owners of these breeds, particularly those that were once used for livestock, but were now bred primarily for show and as pets. The organization has grown from about 15 members at its inception to roughly 120 today. Rorem, the original and current secretary, explains, "We feel that the Border Collie is well served by its [own] organizations and [therefore we] do not presume to set ourselves forward as herding authorities for the breed. However, Border Collies do take part in our events and are very welcome to do so. AHBA events can provide an avenue for involvement in herding for Border Collies [just] as [it does] for other breeds." Those activities include the sanctioning of organized herding tests and all-breed trials.

Health and Breeding

A discussion about health and breeding of the American Border Collie would not be very different from one about the British Border Collie, except in one area. Because no registry in the United States requires that breeding stock be checked and certified free of genetic diseases, the responsibility lies with the breeder. Although eye clinics have been set up at a number of trials in the past few years, participation in them is strictly voluntary and no dog has been known to be excluded from running in a trial whose owner refused to have him tested. While at least one of the registries has agreed to include genetic data on pedigrees when available, its absence has little meaning if it is not a requirement. Furthermore, the existence of more than one registry means that, if they do not all have the same demands, a dog failing the requirements of one may simply register with another. It is therefore imperative that consumers keep breeders honest by scrutinizing the backgrounds of the lines from which they are considering purchasing a dog and by keeping their own standards high.

Border Collies are subject to a number of genetic diseases. *Progressive retinal atrophy* (PRA), an eye disease, is one. A dog with PRA gradually loses its vision as it ages, but may appear normal until middle age. Therefore, there is a possibility that the dog may be used in a breeding program before it becomes symptomatic. ISDS testing has reduced the incidence of PRA in Great Britain, but since there is more than one American registry, none of which requires testing, only breeder responsibility and buyer vigilance can ensure that lines are free from the disease. Most cases of PRA can be detected by the time a dog is two years old. It is therefore recommended that breeding be delayed until then. Breeding stock should also be checked every year after that to be safe.

Another genetic eye disease that can afflict a Border Collie is *Collie eye anomaly* (CEA). Because it is recessive, parents with good vision can pass it on to their puppies. At this time, there is no good way to test the genes of breeding stock, but the lesions produced by CEA can be detected as early as six weeks old, so an entire litter of puppies may be tested, and eliminated from a breeding program if found positive. If missed at six weeks, a dog can be tested, as with PRA, at two years old.

Hip dysplasia (CHD) is another genetic disease on the rise in American Border Collies. It is a common misconception that a dog who is able to work must have good hips. Border Collies are often so engrossed in their

Some people still prefer very classically marked, rough-coated, black-and-white Border Collies like Douglas and Wee Trim, belonging to Jane Porter of Greenacres, Washington.

work they can ignore pain. The Orthopedic Foundation for Animals (OFA) will evaluate hip x-rays and rate a dog. It reports 16.9 percent hip dysplasia in the Border Collie, but since we can assume that in very serious cases the x-rays were not sent to OFA for assessment, this percentage is slanted towards normal. X-rays may be taken of a Border Collie at two years old and sent to OFA for evaluation. Only dogs receiving OFA excellent or good should be considered for breeding.

The notion that poor nutrition and environment alone can cause a dog to become dysplastic is countered by current scientific thought:

"Genetics is the foremost causative factor of canine hip dysplasia. Hip dysplasia is not something a dog gets; it either is dysplastic or it is not. Hip dysplasia is genetically inherited. While environmental effects, including nutrition and exercise, may play a part in mitigating or delaying the onset of clinical signs and clinical symptoms, hip dysplasia remains a genetically transmitted disease. Only by rigorous genetic selection will the incidence rate be reduced." ("Causative Factors of CHD" by John C. Cargill, MA, MBA, MS and Susan Thorp-Vargas, MS, *Dog World*, June 1995.)

While PRA, CEA and CHD are hereditary conditions that can be tested for prior to breeding, or in offspring prior to becoming outwardly symptomatic, others cannot, at least not yet. *Epilepsy*, also known as seizure disorder, is one of these. Incidences of epilepsy are being encountered more and more frequently in the Border Collie. The causes are not yet completely understood, but it appears to run in certain lines. Breeding a dog with epilepsy is not recommended.

Other diseases that may have a genetic component are skeletal problems, and endocrine and immune system diseases. There are enough good working dogs available to breed from in the United States today that it would not be responsible to the future of the breed, to the consumer, or to the reputation of the breeder to use a dog in a breeding program that is at all questionable, no matter what other stellar characteristics you think it has.

Character and Appearance in the American Border Collie

As we have seen, the American Border Collie is essentially the same dog as the Border Collie in Britain and Ireland, but has had a separate history and perhaps been used in different types of working situations. In looks, the breed is identical, and, as we will see, retains the wide diversity that comes about from breeding for herding ability and not for looks. The AKC has a standard for the breed and has had one for years, but since the AKC did not recognize the breed until 1994, there was little need for conformation to its standard. UKC also has a standard that differs somewhat from that of the AKC, but since they do not allow the Border Collie to enter their conformation shows, their standard is only perfunctory. Herding dogs in America, as in Britain, have never conformed to any standard of looks. Many Border Collies are as indifferent-looking today as they were before they became a registered breed. The prevailing thought was that as long as it worked, a working dog need not be considered beautiful. That is not to say that breeders and owners alike have not had their preferences.

Because the Border Collie was originally bred to work under harsh mountain conditions, far away from its handler, the breed had to be intelligent and independent. There have been numerous stories illustrating the working collie's intelligence and independence. Most come from Britain and Ireland where the breed originated, but there are some that are decidedly American. One of my favorites is that told by Enos A. Mills of his collie, Scotch. Mills was a naturalist who did most of his work in the Rocky Mountain range. He acquired Scotch, a black-and-white "old-fashioned collie" puppy, to be a companion, to live with him in his remote cabin and to accompany him on his many treks through the Rockies. But Scotch also "became efficient in driving cattle, horses, and

Karim's Miss Lucy, CDX, TD, a multiple High in Trial obedience winner belonging to Karen Clanin, is "just black-and-white" but her style when working sheep, black face and prick ears give her an entirely different look.

burros", and it turned out, was clever in devising alternate plans when one method didn't work:

"Many of Scotch's actions were beyond the scope of instinct. One of his most remarkable achievements was the mastering of a number of cunning coyotes which were persistent in annoying him. In a sunny place close to the cabin, the coyotes frequently collected for a howling concert. This irritated Scotch, and he generally chased the howlers into the woods. After a time these wily little wolves adopted tantalizing tactics, and while Scotch was chasing the pack one day, a lame coyote broke out in a maddening Babel of yelps and howls. Scotch instantly turned back to suppress him. While he was thus busy, the entire pack doubled back into the open and taunted Scotch with attitudes and howls.

"One night [Scotch] was gone all night. The next morning I was astonished to find another collie in Scotch's bed. Scotch was in a state of worried suspense until I welcomed the stranger; then he was most gleeful. This move on his part told plainly that he was planning something still more startling. That day, at the first howl of the coyotes, both dogs were missing, but presently they came into view, cautiously approaching the coyotes from behind a screen of bushes. Suddenly the visiting collie dashed out upon them. At the same instant Scotch leaped into a willow-clump. While the visiting collie was driving the pack, the lame coyote again came out to make his sneaking flank movement. As he rounded the willow-clump, Scotch leapt upon him. The pack fled and came no more to howl near the cabin." ("The Story of Scotch" by Enos A. Mills, Houghton Mifflin Company, 1909.)

Scotch lived over 80 years ago, but the Border Collie in America today is no less sagacious. In most cases, however, a dog does not get the opportunity today to exhibit its intelligence in quite as dramatic a manner. In most communities, cities, suburban, or rural, a dog cannot be let to run loose; and in most working situations and for trials, owners want a dog under more control. In America, as in the rest of the world, less land is given over to animal husbandry, and fewer farms and ranches are set up to allow a dog to do the work of herding livestock. Earlier, we questioned whether the breed's intelligence would inadvertently be the cause of its demise. If the Border Collie is to survive as a breed in America, it will have to be adaptable. As we have seen, it is a breed that has had a lot of experience with adaptability.

TEMPERAMENT

There has been much concern of late about the Border Collie's temperament. While many Border Collies, even working dogs, live in the home with their human families and are wonderful with children, other pets and visitors, the intensity of a herding dog does not always make for the best choice of a companion. Furthermore, for certain sports, an extremely excitable dog is an asset to be sought out or even bred for, making them less than ideal pets. Some Border Collies are extremely shy or even neurotic unless working. It is important for someone seeking a companion dog, even if it is one that is going to earn its keep as a herding dog, to take these things into account when buying a Border Collie. Ignoring them is the single most recurrent reason why we see so many Border Collies in rescues today. The parents may be seen working or may have trial wins or sporting titles attached to their names, but potential buyers often ignore the temperament of the parents (and grandparents and other offspring) and the environment that the puppies are growing up in.

Even with traditional black-and-white, the possibilities are endless in the Border Collie. This is Tam, a handsome rough-coated dog belonging to Leslie and Michael Tokar of Park Ridge, Illinois.

While with some pups, socialization may not cure inherited character defects, it is equally important for a young dog to be exposed to many

Two of the author's pups inherited the gene for tri-color from their sire, one being the author's red-tri-dog, Woolgather Moss.

different people, a variety of environments, other dogs, children, and different kinds of animals. Many people believe that basic obedience classes are invaluable in this area, and several organizations give training and temperament tests. While not foolproof, these types of early conditioning and opportunities for observation will at least alert an owner to potential problems that can be worked on. The production of sound well-adjusted dogs is a partnership between breeders and owners. So, while we must let breeders know what we expect of them, we also have a responsibility to do our part.

COAT COLOR

Perhaps it's our tradition of independence, or maybe because we are so polymorphous ourselves, Americans seem to embrace the most sundry occurrences of color in a breed that is already so diverse in looks. In Britain and Ireland, black-and-white or tricolored (black, white and tan) prevails. While traditional black-and-white was the color favored by the early handlers and breeders and is still the chief color for Border Collies today, there is no doubt that red (the color called "chocolate" or "liver" in other breeds), which was said to be rare by Pasco in 1937, has become exceedingly popular. Blue merle is sought after and even bred for by some. Predominantly white Border Collies may be frowned upon by shepherds in Britain and Ireland, but here in the United States they have not been all that unusual. Ohio trainer Lewis Pence had a predominantly white bitch with a half-black face in the 1960s, and such colorations are seen frequently today. Along with speckled (dogs born primarily white that develop black speckling throughout the white areas as they mature) and "silver" (dogs that are mostly black, with white speckling), predominantly white dogs are considered "flashy," not only in the obedience ring and on the agility course but on the trials field as

Three-year-old Luzian Thavern With A Twist ("Meghan"), owned by John and Georgia Thomas of Sugarland, Texas, attests to the fact that blue merle is a possibility for a purebred Border Collie.

well (all-white, however, is not acceptable by the AKC standard). Blue ("slate grey") Border Collies are becoming better known, but were not unknown even as far back as the turn of the century, when Andy Little imported some blue dogs into Idaho. Sables are even less rare than blues today and are being sought after. Sable dogs appear most often in the obedience ring, possibly because many are either recent imports from Britain, where sable has been popular in obedience lines, or because they are descended from British obedience lines. The more unusual colors, like fawn (a dilution of liver), ginger (true red), lemon or yellow (dilutions of true red), and brindle, all possible in the Border Collie, are still very uncommon here. Apparently they are better known in Australia, at least among show Border Collies. (*Border Collies* by Joan Bray, Kangaroo Press,

Diane Allevato's Dolly grew up to become a beautiful and interestingly marked sable-and-white Border Collie. Standardization could eliminate the enormous diversity we now see in the Border Collie.

1993.) It will be interesting to see if the more unusual colors actually disappear from American Kennel Club-registered Border Collies as the breed moves closer toward standardization. Some people associate poor herding ability with particular colors, or even with any color except the very traditional black-and-white or tricolor. This phenomenon may be because some breeders ignore working ability and breed poor working specimens just to get the color they want. Consumers should check the herding background of a dog they are considering before buying on color alone. There have certainly been examples of excellent working dogs that sported unusual coat colors, but these were more likely random

Sables are still unusual in the United States, but the variety of beautiful shades and markings possible is likely to make them more popular as people see more and more of them. This is Lady Skye, owned by Noreen Parrel of Rochester, New York.

occurrences of those colors rather than deliberate breeding for them. There is also some concern that certain hereditary diseases are associated with particular coat colors, but until more research is done in the genetics of disease inheritance in dogs, particularly in the Border Collie, we can only speculate. That is not to say, however, that consumers should not make careful inquiries into the apparent health of the lines they are considering.

It goes without saying that Border Collies should not be bred for looks alone. As a working dog, the most important aspects of the breed and therefore the traits most appropriate to breed for are working traits and intelligence. However, once working ability and health of the breeding stock have been satisfactorily demonstrated, there seems to be no reason why one can't indulge one's preferences when choosing a dog. The fact

Lord Rimy, a saddleback sable, belonged to Noreen Parrel.

that we are able to exercise our choice is testimony to the diversity of the breed. We could lose those options if the breed were to be standardized like other breeds.

NAMES

We know that it is common for shepherds to give their working sheepdogs short names. Names like Nell, Cap, Glen, and Meg have become traditional for Border Collies and are also used here in the United States, particularly by shepherds of the older school or traditionalists. In America, however, it seems we are willing to follow custom only so far. So, while short names are still the norm for working Border Collies here, we have expanded the lexicon to include truly American-sounding

Chance has a darker coat (more hairs with black tips) than other sables we have seen. Chance belongs to Sara Bagg, an artist from Tulelake, California.

names like Sioux, Quest, Cody, Tex, Luke, and Pete. These may not seem like customary names to the purist, but they maintain the spirit of the tradition.

Longer more up-beat names, frequently with kennel prefixes, are often given to show or obedience dogs, both here and abroad: Tystar Second Feature, Rivendell's Zip Zap, and Cooperlane Hair Trigger are American Border Collie obedience dogs of note. Kennel names are not unknown in Britain and Ireland, even in trialling. Witness some of the more famous trial dogs — Wiston Cap, Whitehope Corrie or Dryden Joe. But the callname of each of these dogs, Cap, Corrie, and Joe, are incorporated into their kennel names and remain traditional short Border Collie tags. In obedience and show, however, a callname may be entirely different from the full registered name of a particular dog. Whimsical names that appear to violate the spirit of tradition sometimes offend traditionalists by their seeming frivolity, but in context of an obedience trial, or an agility or flyball match, a spirited name may be appropriate. However, they would probably seem completely out of place on the sheepdog trials course, in the pasture or on the hill.

While there are no hard and fast rules, there are certain standards that must be upheld. If a name is embarrassing to say in public, indicates negative behavior or looks, or is likely to be offensive, don't call your dog by it! It might appear amusing at first, but you will probably regret it later.

The Border Collie in Sports

The Border Collie's versatility is what makes it excel in fields other than livestock herding and sheepdog trials. Today, there are many Border Collies winning obedience, agility and flyball matches for their city and suburban owners. These sports, though they may not be classified as "work" per se, cannot be excluded from a discourse on Border Collies in America because of the large number of Border Collie owners in America participating in them.

OBEDIENCE

Obedience originated in Britain and can be traced in the USA to Helen Whitehouse Walker, who first gave demonstrations of obedience in the 1920s. (*Dog Fancy Magazine*, February 1995.) It is a sport in which dogs are trained to perform a variety of exercises on command, with perfection, in competition with other dogs. These maneuvers include walking at heel, long stays, come, down on recall, jumping over hurdles, fetching, tracking and so on, on and off lead. Both the AKC and the UKC give titles to dogs for achieving perfection in this sport. A dog may earn such titles as Companion Dog (CD), Companion Dog Excellent (CDX), Utility Dog (UD) and Utility Dog Excellent (UDX). The highest award in AKC obedience is Obedience Trial Championship (OTCh). Titles are awarded for points earned in numerous competitions, and dogs also compete in each event for achievements such as High In Trial.

Obedience nomenclature is further complicated by the fact that beside the various titles bestowed by the two American kennel clubs, AKC and UKC, Americans may cross the border into Canada and earn Canadian obedience titles as well, and in addition, there are further honors that can be achieved. Local and regional dog clubs hold events, as do two of the largest dog food companies in the United States, Ken-L-Ration and Cycle®, which sponsor regional and national championships every year. Dogs may also earn points toward four honors awarded by *Front and Finish*, a newspaper devoted to obedience training — the Delaney Rating System, the First and Foremost Rating System, the Whitehead Rating System, and Super Utility Dog.

OTCh. Heelalong Chimney Sweep, belonging to Kay and Dick Guetzloff of Phoenix, Arizona.

Border Collies probably have been competing in obedience in the United States since the early '30s. There are a number of established obedience lines in the breed. Dick and Ada Karrasch's Mississinewa Prince Val UDT NA10132 was mentioned earlier. Of him, Nancy Keller says:

"As a sire, Prince Val founded one of the most successful lines of obedience dogs of all times in any breed. Many of the most outstanding obedience dogs in the country claim Prince Val as an ancestor, and he is also behind a number of herding dogs. His daughter, Scherry Star Christy UD was the first of what became known as 'the Louisville Border Collies'. These dogs dominated the Open B and Utility placements at shows in the Louisville, Kentucky area in the late sixties and in the seventies. They were all either descended from or successfully crossed with Prince Val lines." (*The Shepherd's Dogge*, Summer, 1989 and Summer, 1990.)

Lines that have shaped the modern Border Collie in obedience in the U.S.A., such as Scherry Star, Dreamalot, Wondereye and Tystar, all go back to Prince Val and, except for Dreamalot which is largely defunct at this juncture, they are all active today.

Kay Guetzloff is the founder of another line of obedience Border Collies, Heelalong. Born in England, Kay came to the United States in 1965, began in obedience in 1966 and has since earned dozens of obedience and tracking titles in the U.S.A. and Canada. The foundation sire of her line is Imported Heelalong Trevwen Rock AIBC 41482, born in 1980. He was the first imported Border Collie to win Ken-L-Ration Obedience Champion of the Year in 1985. Guetzloff's OTCh Heelalong Chimney Sweep UDX earned Number One in the Top Ten in the Delaney Rating

System for three years in a row and is the highest scoring obedience dog in AKC history with over 6,900 OTCh points, the equivalent of 69 obedience champions. Sweep is also a three-time winner of the Ken-L Ration Obedience Champion of the Year award and the winner of over 150 Highest Scoring Dog in Trial awards. She was bred by Guetzloff, is co-owned and handled by Guetzloff's husband Dick, and is descended from British trialing champions (from Prince Val UDT through Sherry Star lines). Her dam, Heelalong Merrie Meg CDX is the dam of eight obedience trial champions out of three different sires. Kay Guetzloff says of the Border Collie in obedience:

"I don't believe that there is any breed of dog more versatile than the Border Collie. Successful obedience competition requires a willing, agile dog with endurance that likes to work and is quick to learn, and the Border Collie fits all these criteria. Will the Border Collie ever become the top contender in the U.S.A.? I rather doubt it. The Golden Retriever is well entrenched in the top spot. In the United States the rings are small, the exercises are done in the same order every time, and the jumps are always set up the same way. It is very simple for a smart dog to quickly learn the routine. The bright Border Collie is always going to try to come up with a better way to do something.

"Is a very strong herding instinct detrimental to obedience ring performance? I believe it can be. You do see some Border Collies looking at everything other than their handlers. It is not that they are inattentive like many breeds, but more that they have to know what is going on around them at all times. Obedience requires that a dog be totally focused on the handler, and for some Border Collies this is an impossible task." (*The Shepherd's Dogge*, Spring 1992.)

Heelalong is one of the premier obedience Border Collie lines in the country today. Other lines that have achieved fame in obedience with many winning dogs are Somerstar (Whorton/Somerville), Hob Nob (Janice DeMello), Highland (AnneMarie Silverton), Rivendell (Lory Harris Kohlmoos), Wood Glen (Carol Hadnot Crouch) and Norwood

Dawn Jecs of Puyallup, Washington, demonstrating obedience freestyle with OTCh. Checkers during a Cycle® regional tournament.

Dawn Jecs and Strictly Bis-Ness, UD ("Bis") do obedience freestyle in the setting sun.

(Joyce Norris). These provided the genetic foundation for many of today's modern American obedience Border Collies. Many other Border Collie obedience breeders are currently active. Most, however, breed only a few litters, so they have not accumulated large totals of winning dogs from their own breeding. Yet these individuals have a special and important contribution to make to the Border Collie breed in the sport of obedience.

OBEDIENCE FREESTYLE

There is a new sport that has come into being recently and is being entered into by some obedience enthusiasts. Called "obedience freestyle," it resembles nothing better than figure-skating competitions. Cycle® dog food company is the main promoter of this sport and sponsors freestyle competitions at their prestigious Regional and Classic obedience competitions. Obedience freestyle is a dog and handler routine set to music. Costumes are allowed (but no props) and emphasis is on teamwork (between the dog and handler), showmanship, technical precision, originality, and talent of the dog. Not surprisingly, the team that has taken it into the realm of interesting is a Border Collie and his handler, Dawn Jecs of Puyallup, Washington, and OTCh Checkers. Checkers was besides his OTCh and placement at two Cycle tournaments, had been featured in various TV commercials and even starred in his own movie. Along with his celebrity status and obedience career, Checkers was also a certified service dog and demonstrated in the Purdie Prison Pet

Partnership Program in Washington, where prisoners train dogs for seizure alerting and service work for the disabled, which Jecs directed for several years. Jecs also has two other Border Collies that perform in obedience freestyle: Strictly Bis-Ness UD, CGC ("Bis-Kee"), an eight-year-old tricolored male rescue dog that also does flyball and visits nursing homes, and Turn the Page ("Books"), a five-year-old red-and-white male who also gives public service demonstrations and does flyball and herding. Like many Border Collies, Jecs' dogs are extremely versatile and can handle a variety of jobs.

AGILITY

In agility, a dog runs a timed obstacle course. The handler runs with the dog, directing it up, over and through the obstacles consisting of jumps, tunnels, hoops and walks to compete for the fastest course. There are many articles and books that describe each obstacle and the rules of

Agility is a sport that can be enjoyed by both dog and handler as tri-colored Tess of Windy Top, CD and her owner Cynthia Kean of Lockport, New York clearly demonstrate.

the sport, so we won't go into it here. Agility began in Great Britain but has caught on with a vengeance in the U.S.A., so much so that the AKC has now embraced it, with their own course and rules. There are, however, other groups in North America promoting agility—The United States Dog Agility Association (USDAA), the Agility Association of Canada (AAC), the North American Dog Agility Council (NADAC), the Australian Shepherd Club of America (ASCA) and the United Kennel Club (UKC). USDAA, AKC, UKC and ASCA all award agility titles.

The Border Collie is one of the breeds that does extremely well in agility. Unlike in obedience, competitors in America usually do not get Border Collies simply to win at the sport, but many people who have

This handsome red-tri pup, Sweep Bye Ewe ("Scoot"), belonging to Gloria Smith of Newport News, Virginia, is learning to be steady on a version of the "table top" in agility. Scoot has Wiston Cap herding lines on her sire's side and Heelalong Chimney Sweep obedience lines on her dam's side.

Border Collies as pets participate in agility because it is something that can be enjoyed by both the handler and the dog. It is a good outlet for the enormous energy of a Border Collie, being a very physical sport. It is also a competitive team sport demanding good communication between handler and dog, something at which the Border Collie, as a dog bred to work with a shepherd as part of a team, excels.

FLYBALL

Flyball is an all-American dog sport invented in California in the late 1970s. As with most dog sports, Border Collies shine in it. In fact, the Border Collie is the most popular breed in flyball today, with about 25 percent of the nearly 4,000 dogs registered with the North American Flyball Association (NAFA), the governing body in the United States and Canada. To emphasize just how popular Border Collies are for this sport, mixed breeds come in second in popularity with about 10 percent. NAFA was formed in the early 1980s and is considered to be the worldwide authority on flyball. The sport is becoming known in other countries as well, and there is a British Flyball Association.

Flyball is a team sport, akin to a relay race. Each team consists of four dogs and their handlers, with two other dogs as back-ups. A dog races over four hurdles, set at 10-foot intervals, to a box 51 feet from the starting line, and hits the face of the spring-loaded box with its front feet, triggering a mechanism that flips a tennis ball from a hole in the box. Snatching the ball with the side of its mouth, the dog makes a 180° turn and races back over the hurdles to the finish line. It is an uproarious sport, with the audience and handlers all shouting and cheering on the dogs, with the dogs that aren't running at the moment all barking at once. Border Collies love it.

Each successive dog's outward timing must be such that the returning dog crosses the line first. If a dog crosses the starting line early (before the returning dog), it must be re-run after the last dog. Electronic devices

Black-and-white Tam emerges from a tunnel in agility under the watchful eye of his owner Michael Tokar of Park Ridge, Illinois.

("Christmas trees" and "photo-eyes") are now used to determine exactly when a dog crosses the start and finish lines, just like in horse or drag racing. As yet there are no monetary rewards for winning, just certificates, pins, or plaques, but many teams have sponsors, usually a dog food company. NAFA awards titles to the individual dogs on the teams, who earn points toward the titles based on their teams time. Titles are Flyball Dog (FD—20 points), Flyball Dog Excellent (FDX—100), Flyball Champion (FDCh—500), Flyball Master (FM—5,000), Flyball Master Excellent (FMX—10,000), Flyball Master Champion (FMCh—15,000), ONYX award (ONYX—20,000) and Flyball Grand Champion (FGDCh for 30,000 points). To date, six Border Collies have achieved the ONYX title, named after a Doberman Pinscher who was the first dog to achieve the award.

There are quite a few all-Border Collie teams, but often teams like to have a small dog, like a Jack Russell Terrier, chosen for their size and speed, on the team. The height of the jumps is determined by subtracting 4 inches from the shoulder height of the team's smallest dog. A team's time determines the winners of a match, and teams are always competing against their own best time and the current record. Because of this, the record changes rapidly and the winning place gets shuffled around frequently among the best teams.

FRISBEE

The sport of Frisbee was born in the United States in 1974 when 50,000 spectators at Dodger Stadium in Los Angeles jumped to their feet and cheered an uninvited canine athlete named Ashley Whippet, who ran 35 miles an hour, leapt nine feet in the air, and caught Frisbees for eight

Blue-merle Luzian Thavern With A Twist, CDX, NAFDCh, CGC, ("Meghan") easily clears the jumps in flyball. The many titles after her name clearly testify to the versatility of the breed.

minutes before his owner, Alex Stein, was arrested. While a Whippet gave birth to the canine competition that bore his name for years, Border Collies have also been making a name for themselves at the Cycle© Ashley Whippet Invitational Frisbee World Championship, known as the Friskies Canine Frisbee Disc Championship since 1990, when Friskies PetCare Company became the national sponsor. Dogs compete in six regional finals, an Open and the World Championship. In 1984, the winner of the Ashley Whippet Invitational was Peter Bloeme and his Border Collie, Whirlin' Wizard. Wizard is retired now, but Bloeme has produced a video, "Frisbee Dogs Training Video" that features Wizard, a book by the same name, and publishes a newsletter. Don Kent of

Hanover Park, Illinois and his Border Collie, Bandit, have been World Finalists three times. In 1995, Border Collies won in three of the six Regionals, one won the Open, and a Border Collie came in second in the World Championship. Besides competition, Frisbee champions give demonstrations at other sporting events and put on shows for charities.

The sport is a rigorous one, including spectacular leaps, flips and backflips, and requires conditioning and training. Injury is almost inherent in the sport. The twists performed by dogs during leaps may do damage to the spinal column, and hard landings may give dogs similar bone-shattering and compression injuries to those sustained by human athletes. Bloeme has developed a pair of nonskid "sneakers" so that his dog could perform on hard basketball courts, but he recommends that training and demonstrations take place in less punishing grassy areas. The sport looks simple and fun but must be entered with care.

Karen Clanin does Schutzhund with her Border Collies, a sport not usually associated with the breed. Here she is sending out Karim's Kip.

OTHER SPORTS

There are many other dog sports that are traditionally the domain of other breeds that Border Collie owners and their dogs participate in. When one thinks of Schutzhund, German Shepherds and Rottweilers come to mind. However, a number of Border Collies have been successfully trained for this sport, and some are furthermore used in police work where the sport may be put to practical use. Many Border Collies enjoy swimming and retrieving in water, and this skill can be enjoyed in activities generally reserved for Newfoundlands and retrievers. Often clubs that put on sporting events for their own breeds do not restrict entry to only those breeds. Border Collies have been seen in some hunting trials as well. Dog sledding is not limited to Siberian Huskies, Alaskan

Tess of Windy Top, CD, NA, belonging to Cynthia Kean of Lockport, New York, was a member of the Wiz Kids Flyball Team that competes all over the Northeast and Canada.

Malamutes, Samoyeds and other Northern breeds. There are a number of Border Collie owners today who have all-Border Collie sledding teams that even enter some of the larger races.

Skijoring, where a dog pulls a person on cross-country skis, adding to their speed, is a sport akin to sledding, but can be participated in by any dog over 30 pounds that likes to pull. Many Border Collies do or can be trained to. It is an inexpensive sport that can be enjoyed by one person with one or several dogs. The dog wears a harness and a 7 to 12 foot line connects it to a special belt worn by the handler. As with herding, verbal directional commands must used to give the handler control. Mari Hoe-Raitto from Alaska originally got Border Collies for skijoring because she wanted a dog that could be a companion as well. She says that Huskies are kept outside in Alaska, and are not good companions. She still owns Huskies, but also has six Border Collies that she trials with in summer and skijors and sleds with in winter. Borders are powerful and fast, she says, though they can't go as long of a distance as Huskies, and they are more easily trained and controlled. Having Border Collies allowed her young son to begin skijoring at the age of three, and he is now winning races.

The fact is there almost isn't anything that a dog can do that can't be done by a Border Collie. Border Collie owners are not known for their humility—in fact, there is a popular automobile bumper sticker that says, "It's hard to be humble when you own a Border Collie!"

Getting Back to Work

The Border Collies of yesteryear were used to work a variety of livestock and were valued for their ability to adapt to the situation at hand. In 1945, Border Collies were purchased by the Canadian government and given special training as reindeer-herding dogs. At the same time, in the southwestern United States, Border Collies were being used to herd Angora goats. Don Bell described American Border Collies "trained to 'back' sheep" in much the same way as Kelpies are trained in Australia:

"At loading dock or any other completely filled pen or corral, the dog which will hop up on and move across the backs of closely bunched sheep, drop down on command and thereby gain position to move the leaders off and thus move the flock is truly an immeasurably useful beast. This 'backing work' is not an unusual assignment—just another of the expected variations in the routine handling of sheep." (*The Sheepman*, 1945.)

Martha McHardy from Victoria, British Columbia has Border Collies that work stock as their regular vocation, participate in sheepdog trials, flyball, obedience, and accompany her to work in her job as an occupational therapist—truly well-rounded dogs. McHardy believes, as do many other Border Collie owners, that the Border Collie's versatility derives from its herding ability, and if that ability is lost to the breed, either through injudicious breeding or the disappearance of working opportunities, versatility will also be lost to the breed. Versatility allows Border Collies to herd a variety of livestock and also to make their mark in fields that might not always be recognized as traditional "working" realms.

SEARCH AND RESCUE

Search and Rescue often requires a trained team of dog and handler to go into a disaster area—perhaps an avalanche, an earthquake, a plane crash, or the site of a bombing—and search through debris, wreckage, heavy snow, swamp, wilderness or woods, looking for injured people, lost children, dead bodies, etc. Dogs have been used for this purpose for many years—the Saint Bernards of Switzerland are a prime example— and have been used in recent years in highly publicized operations such as the explosion of PanAm Flight 103 over Lockerbie, Scotland, the San Francisco earthquake, and the bombing in Oklahoma City. "Dogs are sent into the worst area," according to Susan Bulanda of Pottstown,

Susan Bulanda's Ness, a very successful search and rescue dog.

Pennsylvania, an author, animal behaviorist, and SAR trainer, "because that is where they can contribute most to the search effort."

Border Collies, who already have a reputation for rescuing shepherds lost in hill fogs or sheep buried in deep snow, are excellent choices for the job of SAR. Bulanda says:

"This type of work requires a dog that is highly motivated to do his job and will stick to the work no matter how difficult and unpleasant. Border Collies fit the bill. Their agility allows them to maneuver easily, their intelligence makes them easy to train, their good nose gives them the ability to do the work, and their desire to work keeps them going. My husband and I both prefer the Border Collie for SAR because of the smaller size, which makes the dog easier to transport and allows it to get into spaces that a larger dog can't go: the dogs live for the work. [They] are able to work well into their later years, and when you consider that it takes at least a year to bring a dog up to operational status, longevity in a dog is an important consideration." (*The Shepherd's Dogge*, Fall 1991.)

Bulanda's dog, Ness NA29761, a grandson of Gilchrist's Spot 24981, was the first documented Border Collie to be used for SAR in this country. He retired at 15 years old and died at almost 16. He was so impressive as a young SAR dog that now many people are using Border

Collies for this important work. Bulanda points out that, while her dogs regularly work stock as well, it takes a strong handler to train a dog for both kinds of work, and she tries to dissuade most people from trying to do both. Dogs with strongly focused herding instincts will not do well in SAR because they put livestock above all else. She recommends training a dog for SAR before taking them to stock. In a search, a dog must have his priorities straight, and a dog that cannot stay on track, even when searching near or through a herd of cattle or a flock of sheep, is useless for SAR.

THE BORDER COLLIE AS SERVICE DOG

Dogs and other animals have been employed for a very long time providing some kind of service to people with physical disabilities. Witness Seeing Eye dogs, which have been accepted as useful in that capacity for many years and their training institutionalized early in this century. It has only been in recent years, however, that dogs have been used to help people with a wide variety of physical problems, or that

DeeDee, belonging to Betty Luttier of Seminole, Florida, is a participant in a pet-facilitated therapy program. Here she visits residents of a nursing home.

studies have been done that indicate pets can be useful in facilitating healing in general. Throughout the U.S.A., organizations have sprung up in recent years whose specific purpose is to utilize dogs for pet-facilitated therapy or as service dogs of one kind or another. Some are purely local, for a single county, town, or even hospital. Others are area-based or national. The larger organizations sometimes breed their own dogs, or acquire young dogs as puppies to train specifically for particular requirements, like Seeing Eye dogs. Other agencies often make use of interested people working with their own dogs. They may provide training for an owner and dog or require that owner and dog pass a

Many Border Collies take quite naturally to the water. Claire Jones's farm-bred Cassie from Alexandria, Kentucky is one of these.

temperament test, or may simply act as clearing houses to hospitals and nursing homes that participate in a pet-therapy program. In other cases, hospitals sometimes allow a single volunteer to come to the hospital with their dog and interact with patients. So many of these groups now exist that it would require a book of its own to cover the topic adequately.

Suffice it to say that Border Collies are among the dogs being used for these purposes because of their temperament, trainability, and "work ethic." While the larger breeds are still sought out most frequently as

Sable Border Collie Skye is retrieving a dummy from the water. This beautiful dog belonged to Noreen Parrel of Rochester, New York.

Seeing Eye dogs mainly due to their size, there are many cases of Border Collies being used for this work. The Guiding Eyes for the Blind, Inc. in New York State utilized Border Collies for Seeing Eye dogs for many years, and one New Hampshire breeder always donated a puppy from each litter to them. Size requirements may also prevent most Border Collies from being used to pull wheelchairs, but again, there are documented cases of larger Border Collies specifically sought out for this work.

Organizations that train "hearing-ear" dogs often choose small to medium-sized dogs, and Border Collies are frequently employed in this capacity. Dogs for The Deaf, a national training and placement organization for hearing-ear dogs, looks for dogs with stable temperaments, confidence, high energy levels, and a strong desire for work, traits that Border Collies usually possess. Dogs are trained to respond to sounds, such as door knocks, door bells, fire alarms, telephones, alarm clocks, oven buzzers, baby cries or people calling out their owner's name.

Jib is one of Susan Bulanda's search and rescue dogs.

OTHER ORGANIZATIONS THAT GIVE WORKING CERTIFICATES

Clever Canine Companions Working Registry was created to give working opportunities to all dogs, combined with education and responsible ownership, by bestowing titles on dogs that achieve some degree of competence in a variety of work categories. The titles include Versatile Canine Companion (VCC) and Versatile Canine Companion Excellent (VCCX). Categories a dog may earn titles in include Health, Obedience, Tracking, Herding, Protection, Draft Work, Soundness (which includes things like Endurance, Hiking, and Agility), and Other (which includes Hero Dog, Therapy Dog, and just about anything not covered by other categories). The point is to encourage people to get out and work with their dog rather than being content to allow their dog to lie about the house all day. Once again, it isn't surprising that one of CCC's two Top VCCX Dog of the Year awards (presented for extra work) in 1992, and the O-VCCX (Outstanding Dog) awarded in 1993, went to a Border Collie,

The author's dogs, Jute and Willy, both working sheepdogs, often enjoyed swimming after sticks thrown into the water for them.

Ness, owned by Susan Bulanda, for Search and Rescue missions and earning herding and tracking degrees. Ness was also a therapy dog, registered with both Therapy Dog, Inc. and Therapy Dog International, two organizations that certify dogs in this important field, where even temperament is important.

Affiliated with CCC is the Water Education & Training Dog Obedience Group (WET DOG). They administer a water rescue test and award three titles: WETT (Wet Dog Tested), WETX (Wet Dog Excellent) and WTXX (Wet Dog Double Excellent). They emphasize that the dog and handler work as a team, and in order for a dog to obtain WTXX the owner must be trained in CPR. The program is open to all breeds, and since most Border Collies enjoy swimming and retrieving in water, this is another activity for them to enter.

Like the livestock-herding degrees given by the National Stock Dog Registry and the American Herding Breed Association, the AKC bestows herding titles: Herding Tested (HT), Pre-Trial Tested (PT), Herding Started (HS), Herding Intermediate (HI), Herding Excellent (HX) and Herding Champion (HCh). Prior to acceptance into AKC, the Border Collie was excluded from earning these titles, but now that it is "official," it may participate in AKC herding events along with the other AKC Herding breeds. It must be said that many herding people consider the AKC herding program to be misleading, its tests inadequate, and its titles given to dogs that could never complete a "real" sheepdog trial course or do a day's work. They fear that owners of dogs with AKC titles after their names will advertise them as producing working offspring and thus

Ferguson's Bawbee could herd the kids as well as the adults. A strong dog can face down even an aggressive adult, but both kids and lambs must learn to fear a dog, and therefore often ignore a strong herding dog.

dilute the gene pool with deficient lines. It is a point well taken and will require vigilance on the part of the consumer to recognize the realities of the dogs they are considering buying. However, *caveat emptor* has always been the byword for those seeking good working stock dogs, and a degree of any kind or registration or membership in any organization is no guarantee of herding ability.

HERDING A VARIETY OF LIVESTOCK

As we have seen, Border Collies have been used all along in America to herd various types of livestock. Dairy farmers choose Border Collies because they work quietly and can move cows at a reasonable speed so as not to upset their milk production. Cattle ranchers also want a calm worker that won't run the weight off their beef cattle. Dogs that fit the bill can be both gentle and aggressive, and know which approach is required. However, Foy Evans, a well-known Border Collie trainer from Arkansas, says:

"The dairy cattle dog and the beef cattle dog are very different in natural ability and training. They may be from the same litter, but the

Bawbee herded a variety of poultry.

Some Border Collies will herd anything that moves. The author's dog Willy was primarily a sheepdog, but loved to herd poultry all his life.

dairy dog does better if he has a 'softer' disposition. The beef cattle dog has to be long on courage and aggressiveness. The training will vary somewhat, too." (*Dog Sport*, June 1980).

Today some American breeders are advertising "Border Collies with bite," possibly to compete more successfully with McNabs and Australian Shepherds, which have a reputation for being stronger workers than Border Collies. Because many farms, particularly in the Northeast, are small and diversified, herding dogs are required to herd everything from chickens to pigs. Many Border Collies enjoy bringing in free-range

Bawbee, who belonged to Margay Ferguson of Wingdale, New York, was a farm dog that herded a variety of livestock, including Angora goats.

hens for the night or swimming in the pond to round up the ducks. This may sound like play rather than work, but on a small farm jobs of this sort are a requirement. The author's own free-range hens used to roam the entire neighborhood's backyards, and it took two working dogs to find them in the wooded and brushed-over area and bring them back at night.

Margay Ferguson of Wingdale, New York described her Border Collie, Bawbee, who worked a variety of poultry and Angora goats on her Teasle Hill Farm:

"She does all the chores with me. When herding poultry (geese, ducks, chickens) she knows that working too close doesn't work, so she relieves the pressure by pretending to find something to eat while keeping them moving along. She is invaluable when handling Hannibal, my Angora buck. She keeps him away from me so that I can accomplish things. She just 'clacks' her teeth (like a woodchuck), lurches toward him, backs up, and repeats this until he backs off. Her agility and aggression toward him are totally different from her gentle handling of the does and kids."

With livestock, each species is different, and sometimes there is even a difference between the males and females of a single species, so that a dog must be able to adapt quickly to be able to work them all. Border Collies are equally at home working Angora goats on large tracts of land in Texas as on small farms in the Northeast. Border Collies on farms throughout the U.S.A. are herding pigs and turkeys. Unusual livestock that is becoming popular on American farms, such as buffalo, ostrich and emu, is being herded by Border Collies as well. Some types of

Jennifer Maginnis's "Shep" herds buffalo carefully in Lithonia, Georgia.

Martha McHardy and her Border Collie, BendAcres Nick, herding a large flock of sheep on "cut-block" acreage in British Columbia.

livestock are much more difficult to work than sheep or cattle and take a tough dog with initiative to figure out how to deal with them. Jennifer Maginnis of Lithonia, Georgia explains that the buffalo she and her husband raise are extremely wild and dangerous: "A dog must learn to swing out wide and come in very low behind their heels or they will get kicked badly, and to avoid the horns and head." David Stephens of Marion, Indiana uses Border Collies to work a large variety of exotic livestock on his Indiana farm. At any time he could have emu, ostriches, alpaca, rhea, and fallow and sitka deer. He says:

"Using a dog to move adult ostriches can be more trouble than it's worth a lot of times. I usually use a tough dog that I will lie down at the edge of a field so he can come in if he sees me in trouble. To move an ostrich with a dog, [the dog has to] come in and really butt into them, then let off when they move away a bit. We [also] use the dogs to exercise chicks. The legs will bow and cripple on chicks with high-protein feed if they get fat too quick. If you move them around every day, giving them 20 minutes of quick exercise it keeps the legs from bowing. An ostrich chick will grow a foot a month and gain about 20 pounds. At three months they will be up to 4 feet tall and weigh 50 to 75 pounds. Without exercise they won't stand that weight." (*The Working Border Collie*, September/October 1994.)

Being able to herd a variety of livestock has other uses as well. When the U.S. Fish and Wildlife Service began a recovery program for Aleutian Canada geese in the 1970s, it took a large number of people two weeks to round up 120 of the endangered birds on Buldir Island off the coast of Alaska in order for biologists to examine, tag and move them to other islands for breeding. In 1989, with the help of two Border Collies, 143 birds were rounded up in just four days. Using quietly working dogs proved less stressful to the geese, and the successful program was repeated in subsequent years, resulting in an increase in numbers for the species, and an upgrade in status from endangered to threatened.

The ability to herd geese is also coming in handy for Border Collies for another reason. Canada geese are attracted to golf courses in large numbers in the United States because most of our manicured golf courses offer water in the form of ponds (water hazards) and large areas of lush grazing (the greens). To wildlife enthusiasts this may seem a blessing, but to course superintendents and golfers, 500 to 1,000 birds grazing on a single course is messy and troublesome. Wildlife conservationists are not too happy about the situation either because some flocks of geese are giving up their patterns of migration to stay at golf courses all year 'round, and, since some golf courses surround reservoirs, health officials are becoming alarmed at the potential for pollution that so many birds may represent. In 1994 the Redding Country Club in Connecticut pioneered a program to use Border Collies to chase off the geese. A dog will accompany ground crews on the seat of a golf cart. As the crew perform their daily tasks, the dog keeps an eye out for geese and herds them away from popular areas. It is just enough harassment to the geese to make them leave for good and seek other havens. Now other golf courses in the country are beginning to employ Border Collies, opening up another avenue of potential for working dogs. Recently a dog rescued by the North American Border Collie Rescue Network member was retrained and placed with a golf course attendant, and several other golf course managers have applied to NABCRN members for rescue dogs. Golf courses are thus becoming a valuable rescue resource as well. Many rescue dogs don't show the strong herding ability needed to herd livestock on farms and ranches or to compete in trials, but have enough to get them in trouble in suburban settings. Herding geese on a golf course may be an obvious outlet for their energy and instincts.

Quiet working dogs prove to be less stressful for geese.

Conservation seems like a perfect modern solution to the dwindling number of actual working situations available for the Border Collie. In Canada, public pressure on the forest industry to adopt more environmentally friendly methods of managing forests has led to using sheep to graze the clear-cut forests of British Columbia. The program was begun in the early 1980s and by 1993 over 32,000 sheep were grazing on thousands of hectares of replanted forest. Sheep keep down weeds, but must be managed to keep them from developing a taste for seedlings. To do this, high-quality forage is planted along with the seedlings, and shepherds are hired to monitor the grazing conditions and move the sheep appropriately. The shepherds use mostly experienced Border Collies with strong herding instincts, natural balance, and an ability to make decisions while out of the handler's sight. In some cases, the tracts being grazed are very remote, very steep, and extremely wild. Under these conditions, several shepherds will be hired for the job, bringing with them as many as ten Border Collies, as well as guard dogs to protect against grizzly bears.

Border Collies can work in the roughest country. McHardy and Brynjac Kelly, Can. CD, Can. SSD, DSD, FlCh. take a break from cutblock shepherding.

Martha McHardy and her dogs have worked in the British Columbian forest management program for a few years, and in 1995 she participated in another Canadian conservation program. In "Urban Grazing," she and her Border Collies drove 400 sheep onto the grounds of the regional park system in the city of Fort Saskatchewan, Alberta, grazing boulevards and various other areas. Keeping the sheep on the unfenced lawns and away from traffic was the daily job of the dogs. Besides the obvious value for turf management, the program brought an unexpected boost to the city's tourist industry, a valuable asset. Also tried in the Edmonton, Alberta City Park System, this program brought a shepherd and four Border Collies to herd 600 sheep-grazing picnic sites and other shared recreation areas. Both these programs have been successful in Canada and have potential for the United States as well.

Border Collies in the Media

   While handlers and their dogs once went to work in motion pictures to promote the breed, today the opposite situation is occurring. More and more Border Collies are obtaining jobs as models and actors due to the Border Collie's newly found popularity. What American Border Collie enthusiast hasn't seen "Mike the Dog" in the movie *Down And Out in Beverly Hills*? Or the Border Collie mother and pups in the hit movie *Babe*? Some are also alarmed by the frequency of appearances of the breed in advertising, but owners whose dogs are being employed in this capacity feel differently, seeing these as new working opportunities for the breed. Sandy Swanson, of Elk River, Minnesota, has a dog that has been in

Border Collies, with their sharply contrasting colors, are nothing if not photogenic. These two cuties are Nellie and Dollie, belonging to Carol Harding of Manchester, Michigan.

Modeling was among the many talents of OTCh. Checkers, owned by Dawn Jecs of Puyallup, Washington.

several national ad campaigns, including one for the Windsor Canadian Company, a whisky producer, and the Northwest Life Insurance Company. The dog's name is Don and he was bred from working lines by Charles O'Reilly of Red Wing, Minnesota. Of Don, Swanson says:

"To us, Don is a special dog. He is a quick learner. We usually get a call about 10:00 pm the night before telling us we have a job for the next morning. My favorite late night call was for an industrial video. We had that night to teach him seven tricks. Don said 'No problem!' and learned all seven. You may have seen him in magazines or on a TV commercial. You may have even seen him in catalogs getting hugged by kids. We feel very lucky to own Don. He always makes us look so good and saves the day."

Border Collies as Pets: An Epilogue

We often hear that a Border Collie does not make a good pet. Bred for intelligence and working ability, the Border Collie can become bored and destructive if not given the attention and exercise he needs. However, we cannot overlook the fact that there are many Border Collies in this country that *are* pets. Often their owners attest to the observable phenomenon that Border Collies *do* make good pets! On the face of it, this appears a contradiction. How can this be?

Tasha and Lucas, belonging to Tom and Gloria Vence of San Carlos, California, come from a herding background, but are themselves pets. Their "jobs" are beloved companions and herders of tennis balls. Pet Border Collies will thrive in these situations as long as their owners take seriously their need for companionship and mental and physical activity.

Rosie with her Nylabone® Frisbee, a beloved pet of John and Joanne Muzyka.

These two are Simon and Cody, belonging to Katie Banks of Chicago. Simon is a rescue dog. Often dogs coming into Border Collie rescue are incredibly handsome specimens of the breed. One wonders how anyone can give them up.

Border Collies that make good pets have owners that make good owners. These owners are devoted to their dogs and devoted to the breed. Things that other people might find irritating in a Border Collie—being compulsive, constantly being "busy," herding the cat or a young child, chasing anything that moves, jumping up the minute the owner gets up to follow them around, and so on—these owners find charming. Many go out of their way to give their dogs a job. We have seen that they take up sports or herding themselves so that their dogs have something to do. Over and over again, the people who sent photographs for this book expressed how wonderful they thought their dog was, how lucky they felt to have a dog like this, how they could never again have another breed of dog. Many of them had stories about their dogs worthy of all the "Old Shep" tales that ever came out of Great Britain and Ireland. Who can tell people like this that the Border Collie does not make a good pet?

However, we owe it to the breed, to its working heritage and versatility, to let potential owners know that the Border Collie is first and foremost a working dog. Adaptability has stood it in good stead throughout its career. Many people seek it out for its intelligence; however, it will be the intelligence of its owners and breeders that will be the deciding factor in the Border Collie's future in America.

Above: Rosie, owned by John and Joanne Muzyka. *Below:* Border Collies can make endearing pets as well as work mates.

Appendix 1:

SHEEPDOG TRIALS

To help you appreciate some of the finer points of the trials, and to make them more interesting for you, we give you the following brief description of the competitors and the origin of the Society.

The first international trials were held at Gullane in Scotland in 1906 and, except in the war years, have continued annually since. In recent years there has been a 'national' trial held in each of the three countries, England, Scotland and Wales, at which 12 competitors from those countries were chosen to represent their country, but in 1961 a new departure was made and a national trial was held in Northern Ireland, and three competitors from this trial went forward to the qualifying trial. In 1965, the Republic of Eire was added and there were four competitors from Ireland including the Isle of Man in the qualifying trial, making a total of 40 dogs from the four countries.

1976 saw the introduction of yet another variation in that in both the national and international trials, the special class for hired shepherds has been discontinued, and shepherds and farmers alike compete in one combined 'singles' class. The national teams have now been increased to 15 each from England, Scotland, and Wales, and 8 from Ireland (including the Isle of Man) making a total of 53 competitors in the qualifying trials for the Supreme Championship.

To be eligible to enter a national, the dog must be entered in the Society's Stud Book before 1 June of the year of the trial. The 15 highest pointed dogs in the English, Scottish and Welsh national and the 8 highest pointed dogs in the Irish national are automatically the team for the 'international' which visits Scotland, England and Wales in turn. The dogs competing in the international are much sought after wherever sheep are to be found, and their progeny are shipped all over the world. It is interesting to mention that money cannot buy entry into the international—the honour must be won at a national.

As far as possible, the conditions and work to be encountered in everyday shepherding on the hills and farms are followed in these trials. On Thursday, following the 'brace' event, and for all of Friday, the qualifying trials are run on a national course. Five sheep are liberated some 400 yards from the shepherd and his dog. The latter is directed to bring the sheep and goes off on a wide 'outrun'. The object of the dog running 'wide' (on to the outside of the course) is, theoretically, to move sheep inside his run toward the middle ground so that when he 'lifts' the main flock stragglers can be quickly and easily collected, whereas had the dog gone directly, they would have been driven away from the flock.

Having completed the 'outrun' the dog quietly arrives behind the 'flock' and waits momentarily for them to settle. Then he approaches and 'lifts' (moves) his charges towards the shepherd, bringing them steadily in the most direct line to his master. When the sheep reach the shepherd the gathering is completed. He then directs the dog to move the sheep behind him and then forward and through a pair of hurdles 150 yards away and 21ft. apart. He then turns them across the field where again 150 yards away is a similar obstacle. Through this, turn again and back to the shepherd where, in a 40 yard circle, the man and dog combine to shed (separate) two sheep from the five. Three sheep are unmarked and two are marked with red collars. It is any two of the unmarked sheep which have to be shed and controlled by the dog.

This accomplished (and not until it is) and the sheep reunited, the shepherd proceeds to a pen 9ft. x 6ft. one 6ft. side of which is hinged and acts as a gate. He keeps the gate open by holding the end of a 6ft. rope and then directs the dog to work the sheep into the pen. The shepherd must remain at the end of the rope to ensure the dog does the major part of the work. Once penned (and consequently mixed up) the sheep are brought back to the ring where the dog has to separate one sheep from the rest. This time it is either of the two sheep with collars and the whole job has to be done in 15 minutes.

On Saturday the course is increased to 800 yards and the number of sheep increased to two lots of ten. The dog must go out on the right or left side as instructed, and gather the first lot, bring them through the gate and return on the other side to gather the second lot, and then unite the two lots and bring them to the shepherd and continue as in the earlier description up to the shedding ring. Here in the 40 yard wide circle five sheep marked with collars have to be shed off from the remainder and then penned. The 'single' is done away with and the time limit is 30 minutes.

Marks are awarded in each section of the work—outrun and lift, fetch, drive (the triangular bit through the gates), shedding, penning, and singling, and in each phase the manner in which the dog does its work and obeys the commands are of great importance. One might mention as an example, that a dog which moved sheep steadily and quietly without too many commands, but was unfortunate in missing the 'gate' might conceivably get more marks than the dog which got the 'gate' but rushed the sheep hither and thither and required a lot of commands. It is the manner in which the work is done which really counts, though the missing of a gate inevitably brings a penalty.

In addition to the single dog classes, there is a class for doubles or brace (two dogs) working, which takes place on Thursday. The work follows the same course except that they work on 10 sheep and are required to pen two lots of 5 on opposite sides of the field. The pens have openings only 5ft. wide and no gate and the dog which pens first has to remain in charge of that pen, whilst the shepherd and the second dog pen in the second five in the other pen.

The whole of the trial is of a practical nature and the International Society does not encourage freak obstacles and circus tricks, but is solely concerned with the practical working capabilities of the Border Collie and his Master.

Appendix 2:

INTERNATIONAL SHEEP DOG SOCIETY

STUD BOOK RULES

Name

1. The Stud Book shall be known as the "International Sheep Dog Society's Stud Book", and will be kept by a Keeper and be managed by a Committee appointed by the Council of the International Sheep Dog Society.

Persons Eligible to use the Stud Book

2. Any Member of the Society who is of good standing is eligible to register dogs.

3. Only persons who are Members of the Society shall be entitled to make application for registration of any particulars in the Stud Book.

Subscriptions (subject to variation by the Council):—
   (i) Entrance Fee £3
   (ii) Annual Members £5

Dogs Eligible for Registration

4. (a) Dogs which are the progeny of Registered Border Collies.

(b) Dogs which, in the opinion of the Stud Book Committee are of sufficient working merit and breeding to justify their registration.

(c) All dogs (except those registered under (b) above) **must be registered by the breeder within six months of birth, or thereafter only on the payment of penalties.**

(d) Puppies born from dual matings will not be accepted for registration.

Records

5. (a) The owner of a dog is required to forward notice, within fourteen days of mating, of every service on a printed form supplied by the Keeper of the Stud Book, and this will be acknowledged by the Keeper. This acknowledgement will be the only proof acceptable to the Society in the event of any dispute or doubt as to the sending of a mating notice by a Member. No mating notice will be accepted unless the Sire and Dam are registered at the time of mating.

(b) On or after 31st December in each year, every Member owning registered dogs shall, if required, furnish the Keeper with a return showing any change in ownership or deaths, and the trial-course and breedings records of all dogs in his possession during the year.

(c) The Society reserves the right to refuse any application for registration at their sole discretion without assigning any reason for such refusal.

(d) Names once used for dogs registered cannot be changed, and should be appropriate to the sex.

(e) Names should be short, and should be capable of being used for the dog whilst working.

Registration Certificates

6. When a dog is registered, the Keeper shall issue to the applicant a certificate of registration.

NOTE — All Border Collie puppies MUST be registered within six months of birth by the Breeder (except registrations under Rule 4 (b).), or thereafter only on the payment of penalties.

A. Philip Hendry, 64 St. Loyes Street,
Bedford MK40 1EZ
Telephone: Bedford 52672

Fees

7. No application or notice shall be registered and no certificate shall be issued by the Keeper until the appropriate fees are paid.

The fees are as follows:—
(a) For dogs born and registered within six months of birth by the **Breeder.**

1.	If BOTH parents are registered as PRA/CEA free.	£ 3.00
2.	If one parent is tested and one parent under two years of age:..	£ 5.00
3.	If one only, or neither parent is so tested.	£10.00

(b) Registrations on merit and breeding (registrations on Merit must be supported by documentary evidence from the Secretary of Local Trials) and proof of having been examined and found free of P.R.A., by a Society approved vet. .. £50.00

(c) Transfer of ownership .. £ 2.50

(d) For registration and exclusive use of prefix or suffix. .. £20.00

(e) For a dog's complete five generation pedigree, including search fee .. £11.00

(f) For a dog's three generation pedigree .. £ 5.50

8. All applications, notices and returns shall be made on official forms to be obtained from the Keeper of the Stud Book free of charge. No application, notice or return shall be registered and no certificate shall be issued by the Keeper until the appropriate forms are officially verified and accepted.

9. The Committee may appoint any Director of the Society, or any Member of the Judges' Panels, as an Inspector to visit the kennels of any Member registering dogs, for the purpose of verifying any of the particulars on registration forms, and all Members shall afford such Inspector every reasonable facility for this purpose.

Penalties

10. Where any applicant for registration makes a false statement or fails or unreasonably delays to give any notification or return required by these rules, the Stud Book Committee shall be entitled to refuse registration and have the registration of any dogs owned by the Member cancelled.
The following penalties are payable by the owner of the bitch if the dogs are not registered within six months of birth:—

(a) If registered between the sixth and ninth month of birth a penalty of £11.00 per pup.

(b) If registered between nine months and two years of birth a penalty of £16.50 per pup. Such cases to be referred to the Stud Book Committee.

(c) Application for registration of dogs over two years will be rejected.

11. The Council of the Society may also expel from Membership of the Society any person contravening these rules.

12. The Owner of any dog failing to render a mating card to the Keeper of the Stud Book at the proper time shall be held responsible for any financial loss sustained by the owner of the bitch. Where the mating cards are not returned within 21 days the following penalties become payable by the owner of the sire:—

(a) If returned after twenty one days of the mating but before the expiry of four weeks a penalty of £5.00.

(b) If returned after four weeks, but before the expiry of six months, a penalty of £10.00.

(c) If returned after six months a penalty of £15.00.

NATIONAL CHAMPIONSHIPS
1. SINGLES
COURSE

COURSE FOR QUALIFYING TRIALS

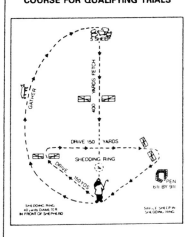

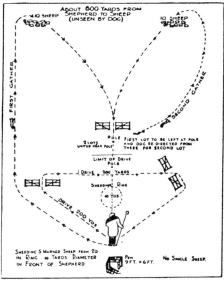

INTERNATIONAL TRIAL. COURSE. FOR SUPREME
CHAMPIONSHIP

COURSE FOR "BRACE" CHAMPIONSHIP

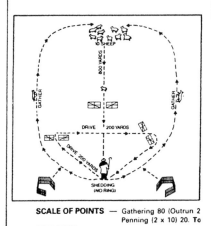

SCALE OF POINTS — Gathering 80 (Outrun 2
                        Penning (2 x 10) 20. To

TIME LIMIT — 25 minutes. No extensi

Appendix 3:

THE KENNEL CLUB STANDARD FOR THE BORDER COLLIE

General Appearance—Well proportioned, smooth outline showing quality, gracefulness and perfect balance, combined with sufficient substance to give impression of endurance. Any tendency to coarseness or weediness undesireable.

Characteristics—Tenacious, hard-working sheep dog, of great tractability.

Temperament—Keen, alert, responsive and intelligent. Neither nervous nor aggressive.

Head and Skull—Skull fairly broad, occiput not pronounced. Cheeks not full or rounded. Muzzle, tapering to nose, moderately short and strong. Skull and foreface approximately equal in length. Stop very distinct. Nose black, except in brown or chocolate colour when it may be brown. In blues nose should be slate colour. Nostrils well developed.

Eyes—Set wide apart, oval-shaped, of moderate size, brown in colour except in merles where one or both or part of one or both may be blue. Expression mild, keen, alert and intelligent.

Ears—Medium size and texture, set well apart. Carried erect or semi-erect and sensitive in use.

Mouth—Teeth and jaws strong with a perfect, regular and complete scissor bite, i.e. upper teeth closely overlapping lower teeth and set square to the jaws.

Neck—Of good length, strong and muscular, slightly arched and broadening to shoulders.

Forequarters—Front legs parallel when viewed from the front, pasterns slightly sloping when viewed from side. Bone strong but not heavy. Shoulders well laid back, elbows close to body.

Body—Athletic in appearance, ribs well sprung, chest deep and rather broad, loins deep and muscular, but not tucked up. Body slightly longer than height at shoulder.

Hindquarters—Broad, muscular, in profile sloping gracefully to set on of tail. Thighs long, deep and muscular with well turned stifles and strong well let down hocks. From hock to ground, hindlegs well boned and parallel when viewed from rear.

Feet—Oval, pads deep, strong and sound, toes arched and close together. Nails short and strong.

Tail—Moderately long, the bone reaching at least to hock, set on low, well furnished and with an upward swirl towards the end, completing graceful contour and balance of dog. Tail may be raised in excitement, never carried over back.

Gait/Movement—Free, smooth and tireless, with minimum lift of feet, conveying impression of ability to move with great stealth and speed.

Coat—Two varieties: 1) Moderately long; 2) Smooth. In both, topcoat dense and medium textured, undercoat soft and dense giving good weather resistance. In moderately long-coated variety, abundant coat forms mane, breeching and brush. On face, ears, forelegs (except for feather), hindlegs from hock to ground, hair should be short and smooth.

Colour—Variety of colours permissible. White should never predominate.

Size—Ideal height: dogs; 53 cm (21 in); bitches slightly less.

Faults—Any departure from the foregoing points should be considered a fault and the seriousness with which the fault should be regarded should be in exact proportion to its degree.

Note—Male animals should have two apparently normal testicles fully descended into the scrotum.

American Kennel Club Standard for the Border Collie 211

Appendix 4:

AMERICAN KENNEL CLUB STANDARD FOR THE BORDER COLLIE

General Appearance—The Border Collie is a well balanced, medium-sized dog of athletic appearance, displaying grace and agility in equal measure with substance and stamina. His hard, muscular body has a smooth outline which conveys the impression of effortless movement and endless endurance—characteristics which have made him the world's premier sheep-herding dog. He is energetic, alert and eager. Intelligence is his hallmark.

Size, Proportion, Substance—The height at the withers varies from 19" to 22" for males, 18" to 21" for females. The body, from point of shoulder to buttocks, is slightly longer than the height at the shoulders. Bone must be strong, not excessive, always in proportion to size. Overall balance between height, length, weight and bone is crucial and is more important than any absolute measurement. Excess body weight is not to be mistaken for muscle or substance. Any single feature of size appearing out of proportion should be considered a fault.

Head—Expression is intelligent, alert, eager and full of interest. Eyes are set well apart, of moderate size, oval in shape. The color encompasses the full range of brown eyes; dogs having primary body colors other than black may have noticeably lighter eye color. Lack of eye rim pigmentation is a fault. Blue eyes are a fault except in merles, where one or both, or part of one or both eyes, may be blue. Ears are of medium size, set well apart, carried erect and/or semi-erect (varying from one-quarter to three-quarters of the ear erect). The tips may fall forward or outward to the side. Ears are sensitive and mobile. Skull is broad with occiput not pronounced. Skull and foreface approximately equal in length. Stop moderate, but distinct. Muzzle moderately short, strong and blunt, tapering to nose. The underjaw is strong and well developed. Nose color matches the primary body color. Nostrils are well developed. A snipy muzzle is a fault. Bite: Teeth and jaws are strong, meeting in a scissors bite.

Neck, Topline, Body—Neck is of good length, strong and muscular, slightly arched and broadening to shoulders. Topline is level, with slight arch over the loins. Body is athletic in appearance. Chest is deep, moderately broad, showing great lung capacity. Brisket reaching to the point of the elbow. Rib cage well sprung. Loins moderately deep, muscular, slightly arched with no tuck-up. Croup gradually sloped downward. Tail is set low. It is moderately long, bone reaching at least to the hock. It may have an upward swirl to the tip. While concentrating at a given task, the tail is carried low and used for balance. In excitement it may rise level with the back. A gay tail is a fault.

Forequarters—Forelegs well boned and parallel when viewed from front, pasterns slightly sloping when viewed from side. The shoulders are long and well angulated to the upper arm. The elbows are neither in nor out. Dewclaws may be removed. Feet are compact, oval in shape, pads deep and strong, toes moderately arched and close together.

Hindquarters—Broad and muscular, in profile sloping gracefully to set of tail. The thighs are long, broad, deep and muscular, with well-turned stifles and strong hocks, well let down. When viewed from the rear, hind legs are well boned, straight and parallel or are very slightly cowhocked. Dewclaws may be removed. Feet are compact, oval in shape, pads deep and strong, toes moderately arched and close together. Nails are short and strong.

Coat—Two varieties are permissible, both having soft, dense, weather-resistant double coat. In puppies, the coat is short, soft, dense and water resistant, becoming the undercoat in adult dogs. The rough coat is medium to long, texture from flat to slightly wavy. Short and smooth coat on face. Forelegs feathered. Rear pasterns may have coat trimmed short. With advancing age, coats may become very wavy and are not faulted. The smooth coat is short over entire body. May have feathering on forelegs and fuller coat on chest.

Color—The Border Collie appears in many colors, with various combinations of patterns and markings. The most common color is black with or without the traditional white blaze, collar, stockings and tail tip, with or without tan points. However, a variety of primary body colors is permissible. The sole exception being all white. Solid color, bi-color, tri-color, merle and sable dogs are judged equally with dogs having traditional markings. Color and markings are always secondary to physical evaluation and gait.

Gait—The Border Collie is an agile dog, able to suddenly change speed and direction without loss of balance and grace. Endurance is his trademark. His trotting gait is free, smooth and tireless, with minimum lift of feet. The topline does not shift as he conveys an effortless glide. He moves with great stealth, strength and stamina. When viewed from the side, the stride should cover maximum ground, with minimum speed. Viewed from the front, the action is forward and true, without weakness in shoulders, elbows or pasterns. Viewed from behind, the quarters thrust with drive and flexibility, with hocks moving close together but never touching. Any deviation from a sound-moving dog is a fault. In final assessment, gait is an essential factor, confirming physical evaluation.

Temperament—The Border Collie is intelligent, alert and responsive. Affectionate toward friends, he may be sensibly reserved toward strangers and therefore makes an excellent watchdog. An intensive worker while herding, he is eager to learn and to please, and thrives on human companionship. Any tendencies toward viciousness or extreme shyness are serious faults.

Faults—Any deviation from the foregoing should be considered a fault, the seriousness of the fault depending upon the extent of the deviation.

Approved Date: January 10, 1995
Effective Date: April 30, 1995

Index